Language Readers

Level 3
Book I
Units 49–54

Jane Fell Greene
Judy Fell Woods

Copyright 2000 (Third Edition) by Jane Fell Greene and Judy Fell Woods.
All rights reserved.

05   04   03   02   7   6   5   4

ISBN 1-57035-443-X
ISBN 1-57035-277-1 Set

No portion of this work may be reproduced or transmitted in any form or by any means, electronic or mechanical, including photocopying or recording, or by any information storage and retrieval system, without the express written permission of the publisher.

Text layout and design by Kimberly Harris
Cover design by Becky Malone
Cover Image © *2000 by* Digital Vision Ltd.
Illustrated by Peggy Ranson

This product is in compliance with AB2519 California State Adoption revision requirements.

Printed in the United States of America

Published and Distributed by

SOPRIS
WEST

4093 Specialty Place   •   Longmont, CO 80504   •   (303) 651-2829
www.sopriswest.com

Contents

Unit 49 The Silver Combs 1

Unit 50 The Myth of the Crystal Cypress 21

Unit 51 Dirt Bike Bozo 41

Unit 52 Changes 61

Unit 53 Every Ending is a New Beginning. 83

Unit 54 A Winner Never Quits 103

Unit 49

THE SILVER COMBS

UNIT 49

Phonology/Orthography Concepts

- Phonograms are letter groups that usually represent the same sounds (phonemes).
- At the ends of words, the phonograms **mn** and **mb** represent the phoneme /m/.

Vocabulary

aplomb	crumb	plumb	*canoe*
autumn	dumb	plumber	*carrot*
bomb	entomb	solemn	*shoved*
catacomb	hymn	succumb	
climb	jamb	thumb	
column	lamb	tomb	
comb	limb		
condemn	numb		

THE SILVER COMBS

Story Summary:

Pat and Trish Marks's father, Herbert, loses his job with a big firm in town. They have important decisions to make and Gram Marks helps.

Pat Marks felt numb. She never thought there would come a day when she would have to move away from her home. But that day might just have come. Her father, Herbert, had lost his job. His division of the company had been closed.

Waiting for her father to walk through the door that afternoon, Pat felt drained. She had shed all the tears she had inside. She remembered feeling this way many years ago when her mother had died. She'd had this feeling again last year when her grandfather died. Pat hadn't really thought she could ever feel that bad again, but she did. She felt like a huge bomb had been dropped and she had nowhere to hide.

From the greenhouse windows overlooking the pool and patio area, Pat could see her little sister Trish playing in the giant rain puddles. They were all that remained of last night's thunderstorm. Trish and her friend, Sis Turner, were pretending to be Indian princesses. Adorned with precious jewels and headbands, they were being brought back to their village in ornate canoes. "Dumb kids," thought Pat. "Don't they see what the world's really like?"

Pat recalled how her dad had told her last summer about the recession. Many people were unemployed. But Pat still couldn't believe it when her dad came home and said that he had lost *his* job!

He said everything would be OK. He had always been able to take care of Pat and Trish. That wouldn't change. They wouldn't have to worry about food or shelter. But they probably wouldn't be able to have many of the things they were accustomed to—at least for a while. And they might have to *move*! Pat had tried to explain it to Trish. Trish didn't seem worried, not really bothered by it at all. "Third graders just don't understand anything," Pat thought despondently.

To make matters worse, Pat had just been elected to the student council and the cheerleading squad for next year. She had tried out for the squad last year but had not made it. Now she felt that she just had to go to school in Jasper next year. She just had to.

Suddenly, Trish and Sis tore through the back door to the kitchen like two whirlwinds.

"Can't you two keep it down to a roar?" Pat called out, trying to hide her tears.

"Geez, we're just looking for something to eat," Trish shouted back. "A carrot, a crumb, anything!" The two younger girls laughed and joked while they pulled a bag of carrots from the vegetable bin.

Vaulting into the sunroom, carrots in hand, Trish and Sis leapt up onto the wicker love seat.

"Just look at your sneakers," Pat scolded Trish. "You and Sis are covered with mud. Go back to the foyer and take off your sneakers! Don't you ever notice anything? Where did you get those silver combs? Those are the silver combs Gram gave me. Give them to me now! Did I tell you you could wear them for dress up? NO!" Pat's temper blew like a volcano's fiery spews.

Carefully handing back her sister's silver combs, Trish muttered in a weak voice, "You *did* let me use them last week when we were playing 'Queen of the Nile.' You said if I was very careful I could use them. And I've *been* very careful. Why are you acting so snotty, Pat?"

"Just get out of here and wipe your feet!" Pat needed to talk to someone. Silver combs in hand, she decided to phone

Gram. Her father's mother, Gram Marks, had always been able to calm Pat down. She was the one who had given her the precious silver combs. They had once belonged to Pat's great-grandmother.

Pat's hands trembled as she dialed Gram's number in Wisconsin. How could she explain this to Gram? They were two generations apart. Could Gram ever understand the feelings Pat was having? "Maybe I'm just a spoiled brat who's always had everything she's ever wanted," Pat pondered. Quiet tears dripped like rain from tree limbs after a shower. "Please be home, Gram," Pat wished aloud.

After several rings, Gram's precious voice sounded in the receiver. "Hello. Hello?"

"Hi, Gram!" Pat choked, holding back the tears. "I've got your silver combs in my hand and I'm . . . ."

"Pat, baby lamb, what's the matter? You sound like you've been crying." Gram could always tell.

At once, Pat knew Gram would understand. "Oh, Gram," sobbed Pat, "I'm miserable. This whole thing with Dad losing his job. I mean, what if we have to move? Dad's looking, but he says there's not much chance for him to get a job here in Jasper. Other people have lost their jobs, too. What if we do have to move? I love my home so much, Gram. And my friends and my school. Everything I've worked so hard for is suddenly going down the drain. Will anything ever be the same again?" By now, Pat was sobbing so hard that she could hardly get the words out.

Gram's voice became suddenly solemn. "Pat, you listen to me. Get control of yourself. It's times like these that help make you a woman. Learning to handle problems helps you grow up. You mustn't lose hope. Just because your father lost his job, it doesn't mean the end of the world."

"But I just can't help feeling so depressed, Gram," Pat cried. "I don't want Dad to know how I'm feeling because he'll feel even worse than he already does, and I hate Trish! Trish acts like it's no big deal. How come bad times don't bother her, Gram?" Pat resented Trish's ability to withstand the pressure.

"Trish is just too young to let these things bother her," Gram replied. "Remember what you said about all the things that you had worked so hard to accomplish in your life? Trish just hasn't had time to achieve as much. Her time will come. But let her be for now. She's enjoying her childhood. Be glad that she's not affected by all that's happening around her. Watch and learn from her. Little ones are sometimes the wisest. Their pure and simple ways could help us all in our dealings with everyday strife and pain. Try to understand. It will all work out, Pat. It always does." Gram's words were already sinking in. Pat knew she was right.

"I think I know how *you* are feeling, child," Gram continued, her voice as steady as a rock, "because this sort of thing happened to me as a girl. It was during the big depression of the '30s. My daddy had died while he was working on the railroad. My  Mama, your great-grandmother, and my three brothers and I were living in Kansas at the time. It was such a long time ago. I was just about your age. We had nothing but our dreams back then. But Mama had great strength. It was then that she gave *me* the silver combs. That's when Mama first read us the wonderful poetry of Langston Hughes."

"Oh, we learned about him, Gram!" Pat recalled.

"Well," Gram asked, "have you ever read his poem, *'Mother to Son'?*"

"No," Pat replied. "Can you remember it, Gram?"

"Every word," Gram said with a lilt in her voice. "Just as I told it to your father, when he was your age."

Gram composed her thoughts. Then she recited the poem perfectly to Pat:

Well, son, I'll tell you:
Life for me ain't been no crystal stair.
It's had tacks in it,
And splinters,
And boards torn up,
And places with no carpet on the floor—
Bare.
But all the time
I'se been a-climbin' on,
And reachin' landin's,
And turnin' corners,
And sometimes goin' in the dark
Where there ain't been no light.
Don't you set down on the steps,
Cause you finds it kinder hard.
So, boy, don't you turn back.
Don't you fall now—
For I'se still goin', honey,
I'se still climbin',
And life for me ain't been no crystal stair.[1]

"Oh, Gram, am I just a spoiled brat?" Pat wondered out loud. "I don't want to be. But it's so hard when it feels like I've lost my whole life. It's not that I want to give up or anything. I just hate to lose what I worked so hard to get."

"Then you should be able to understand how your father must be feeling," Gram advised. "He's worked very hard to become the person he is. He has sacrificed and saved and built a very nice life there for you girls. Now he has some important decisions to make and he needs your help and support. You know, he often told your Gramps and me that nothing in the world would ever come before you two girls. Nothing!"

"Oh, Gram, I've been so selfish. You always help me see things clearly. Dad and Trish both need me, don't they? I'm just glad you understand 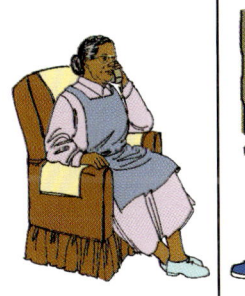 me. I wish I could see you more often. I need to be around you. You're like a doctor's prescription. 'Take two doses of Gram each day! And plenty of water!'" For the first time in a week, Pat had a smile on her face. Gram was her healer.

"I can tell that you're feeling better now, lamb," Gram assured her. "So let me talk to Trish before you hang up. And tell your father to call me if he needs to talk or just wants to chew the fat!"

Pat called Trish to the phone. Just before Trish hung up, Herbert Marks trudged through the back door. His face mirrored his feelings. The late afternoon sun cast a forlorn shadow above the hat he hung on the hook next to the kitchen door. Pat couldn't remember when he had ever looked this bad.

"Hi, precious ones," Herbert sighed, trying to be pleasant. "Who's Trish talking to?" he asked Pat, giving her a kiss on the cheek.

"Hi, Daddy. It's Gram," Pat replied. "I called her a little while ago. I know I probably shouldn't have talked so long, but I really needed to talk to her."

"It's OK, Pat," assured Mr. Marks. "I think I need to speak to her, too. I'll go into the den and pick up the extension."

Pat and Trish had some carrot cake and milk while they waited for their father to hang up the phone. "What do you think they're talking about, Pat?" Trish wondered.

"I don't really know, Trish," replied Pat. "He may just be letting her know how job hunting is going and getting her advice or something."

"Want to play a board game while we're waiting?" Trish begged.

Pat knew Trish loved board games. And even though she could think of a thousand things she would rather do, she agreed.

It was nearly a half hour later when their father set foot in the kitchen. Pat could tell that an important decision had been made. Her dad just looked different. More hopeful, maybe. Contentment filled a space where just minutes before there had been despair.

"Girls," Herbert began with a broad smile. "Let's go out to dinner. I have a proposal to make to you."

"Let's go for fried chicken, Dad," begged Trish. "Please?"

"What kind of proposal?" Pat wanted to know.

"It will keep until we get there," replied her dad.

On the way to the restaurant, they talked about their days at school. It wasn't until they got inside that Herbert announced his proposal. "How would you two girls like to go to Wisconsin and live on Gram's farm?" he asked as casually as if he had just asked for a diet soda.

"Would you go live with us, too?" Trish asked.

"Certainly," Mr. Marks said. "Our whole family would go."

"Wow! Sounds great, Dad!" Trish answered, pausing to think. "I wonder how Star and her new litter of piglets are doing? And the lambs!"

"How about you, Pat?" her dad queried.

"I don't know how I feel," she said worriedly.

"Now I want you two girls to really think about this. I don't mean just for a visit, Trish. I mean that we would live there for a long time. Maybe for the rest of our lives. That is, until you girls decide to go to college or get married or just grow up and want to move away. But it would still be a long time," Herbert went on. "There are no jobs for me here in Jasper. So we can't stay here. The farm would be a great place for us to live. You girls know that I will do just about anything for you, but you have to help me by talking about how you're feeling. We're in this as a family."

"Like I said before, Dad," Trish mumbled, taking a bite out of her chicken drumstick, "I could be very happy on Gram's farm. I love the animals! All kinds of animals. I would feed the chickens and do the chores. Do kids who live on farms have to go to school, Dad?"

"Yes, kitten," her dad said with a grin, "all kids have to go to school. That piece of your life won't change at all."

"But, Dad," Pat blurted, crumbling her biscuit, "that's the very thing that *will* change for me! School! How can I leave now? Next year I'll be a freshman at Jasper High. And I've been elected to the student council and the cheerleading squad. Oh, Dad, can't you see? I'd probably be a drip at a new high school. Kids I don't know at all. People with different attitudes and feelings. Teachers who don't understand me." Pat's emotions exploded.

"Believe me, Pat," her father said solemnly, "I understand your feelings. I have thought and thought about this kind of move and its meaning to you."

"I really don't think you understand at all!" Pat's tension filled the air. "I just don't want to leave . . . ."

Herbert could sense Pat's uncertainty, but he felt he had to rationalize his decision as best he could. "Times are changing, Pat," he explained. "More people are out there trying to do fewer jobs. I feel that saving Gram's farm is the job I need to do now. But it's a decision we'll all have to agree on."

The ride home from the restaurant was long. Pat was subdued. When they got home, she excused herself and went up to bed. Shortly afterward, she heard a soft tapping on her bedroom door.

"Can I come in, Pat?" her dad spoke quietly.

"Sure, Dad," Pat answered. "Sorry about how I acted at the restaurant."

"It's OK. You needed to get it off your chest," her dad inferred. "But now I want you to think about your last conversation with Gramps. We were in Wisconsin for our vacation. And I distinctly heard you telling Gramps that you had always wanted to farm the land. Like our ancestors. And all the Markses to come."

"You're right, Dad," Pat agreed. "I get a funny feeling when I'm on that farm. Trish and I have stayed there every summer. And I know every inch of the farm. Just thinking about it makes me want to go back. I just can't imagine what it will be like having to make all new friends and stuff like that."

"I'm not saying that it would be easy," her father agreed. "Because it will probably be one of the hardest things you'll ever have to do in your whole life. But making a decision and sticking with it—no matter what—will make you a stronger person."

With that, Trish bounced into the room. "How about a family hug?" she asked. "Our family needs one."

While the three hugged, Pat recalled her conversation with Gram. "Gram read me that Langston Hughes poem, *Mother to Son,* today. She reminded me that each time you fall down, you have to pick yourself up."

"Life is not a crystal stair," commented Mr. Marks.

"What's a crystal stair?" Trish asked.

"It's an imaginary stairway that people have to climb to reach their dreams," her dad told her. "It looks as clear as a crystal when people are young, like you, Trish. But when they get a little older, like Pat's finding out, the stairs aren't so crystal clear any more. They get harder and harder to climb. There are obstacles in the path. Some of the steps are made of splinters. And there's no light when you get ready to climb once more."

"But Gram reminded me that people have to keep on climbing those stairs," Pat confided. "They can't sit down. They just have to keep on climbing them if they want to get to the top of their dreams."

"It's like moving away, isn't it Daddy?" Trish asked with the wisdom of a child. "It'll be hard for us to leave our home and our friends. Because we love them. But we can make new friends. And we'll be helping Gram."

"Pat," asked her father, "do you think you can make this move without it ruining your life?"

"I'm not saying I'll be the best person to live with all the time," Pat said honestly, "but I'll give it my best shot. It's going to be real hard to leave all my friends. But I guess you've convinced me that I can make new ones. And, like Trish said, we'll be helping Gram and saving the farm."

After her dad and sister had left, Pat couldn't help but feel a sense of relief. She took the silver combs out of her hair and put them on the dresser—where she could see them again when she woke up. As she drifted off to sleep, she thought about life on a farm. And crystal stairs.

Vocabulary Expansion

Describe and define these words and phrases:

generations to come	wisdom of a child	ruining your life
huge bomb dropped	nowhere to hide	what a shock
recession	hitting the country	accustomed to
despondent	student council	whirlwind
fiery spews	acting snotty	keep it down to a roar
spoiled brat	really getting to me	set foot in
wish out loud	get control	the end of the world
bad times	sinking in	steady as a rock
I'se still climbin'	point of view	depression of the '30s
healer	board game	be a drip

Language Expansion Activities

1. Langston Hughes' poetry is well known. Find a book of his poetry and have a poetry reading with your group. Let everyone in the group choose one of Mr. Hughes' poems and read it aloud for the group. Sit in a circle and discuss Mr. Hughes' poetry. What things about his poems are relevant to your life? Explain.

2. Go to the library and look up the poem, *Mother to Son*, by Langston Hughes. Read the poem through to yourself several times. Rewrite the poem in ordinary, everyday language. Then explain why the language of the poem is so beautiful. What does this poem have to do with the story, *The Silver Combs*?

---

[1] From COLLECTED POEMS by Langston Hughes. Copyright © 1994 by the Estate of Langston Hughes. Reprinted by permission of Alfred A. Knopf, a Division of Random House, Inc.

Language Expansion Questions

1. Why was Pat so distressed? Have you ever been distressed? Explain the circumstances.

2. Describe Pat's feelings. Have you ever felt that way?

3. Trish didn't seem to mind that the family might have to move. Why? What did Gram mean when she told Pat that Trish just hadn't had time to achieve as much? Why would that matter?

4. Why did Pat say that Gram was a healer? Do you know anyone like that? Would it be good to be thought of in that way? Why?

5. Pat was angry because she didn't think her father understood how she was feeling. After they talked about it, she felt better. Why is talking to someone an important step in understanding his or her feelings? Should everyone have someone he or she can talk to?

6. Think about the last time you had a terrible day. Compare your day to Pat's. Decide whose day was worse: yours or Pat's. Why?

7. What if Mr. Marks had found another job in Jasper that day? How would the story have changed? Write a new ending.

8. Judge whether Mr. Marks' decision to move to Wisconsin and help Gram out on the farm was a good one or not.

9. Choose the person with whom you would have the most in common: Pat, Trish, Mr. Marks, or Gram. Explain.

10. Write interview questions for Langston Hughes. What kinds of things would people like to know about him?

Unit 50

THE MYTH OF THE CRYSTAL CYPRESS

UNIT 50

Phonology/Orthography Concepts

In the **middle** of a word, the grapheme **y**:
- Represents long /ī/ with final silent **-e**, consonant **-le**, or in open syllables.
- Represents short /ĭ/ in closed syllables and in one-syllable words.

Vocabulary

acolyte	formaldehyde	Lyme (Disease)	syllable	*nothing*
analyze	gargoyle	lyre	sylph	*answer*
argyle	gypsy	mystery	sympathize	*among*
byte	gyrate	myth	synagogue	
chyme	gyroscope	neophyte	syncopate	
crypt	hybrid	paralyze	syndicate	
crystal	Hyde	psyche	syndrome	
cycle	hydrant	pyre	synopsis	
cyclone	hydrate	rhyme	synthetic	
cypress	hydraulic	rye	system	
dialyze	hyphen	scythe	thyme	
enzyme	hypnotic	style	tyke	
		sycamore	type	

THE MYTH OF THE CRYSTAL CYPRESS

Story Summary:

The myth about a magical crystal cypress tree has been a part of the Jasper community's culture since the time of its earliest settlers. Nobody has ever fully understood it. People in modern times have forgotten it. But Walter Grunch finds meaning in the tree and its legend.

There was a myth the old people told about an ancient cypress tree that stood hidden at the edge of the sea among other, similar cypress trees. They called it the crystal cypress. Long ago, some gypsies drove through Jasper, stopping to ask questions about the crystal cypress and the legend that surrounded it.

A wrinkled old gypsy lady, wife of the leader, had gazed into her crystal ball, seeking a clue to the whereabouts of the magic cypress. There had been no answer. People who had been there in 1959, when the leader of the gypsies entered Ted's Shell Shop, remembered what the old traveler had said to Ted: "When you find the crystal cypress, you will know the answers to all of the questions in the universe." And the gypsies promptly went off in search of the crystal cypress.

For a few days, townspeople had a fleeting interest in the crystal cypress. But the gypsies had only been in town for a few hours, and nothing had happened while they were there. So everyone quickly forgot.

But Mr. and Mrs. Grunch's experience changed that. It began after Mrs. Grunch suffered a heart attack. She told her husband it had felt like a cyclone, whipping through her chest. After two weeks in the hospital, the doctors agreed: Mrs. Grunch needed less work and more rest. They recommended that Mr. Grunch and his wife move out of their rambling old Victorian house and into an efficiency apartment.

Weeks later, the Grunches began packing and discarding the things they had collected during fifty years of living in the house. One afternoon, in the attic of their home, Mrs. Grunch came across a package of letters written by her Aunt Frances to her mother, back in the late '20s.

She untied the fragile blue ribbon that bound the letters together. "I don't remember ever seeing these," remarked Mrs. Grunch to her husband. "I suppose that Aunt Susan packed them away up here after Mama died in the winter of '43. You were away in World War II then."

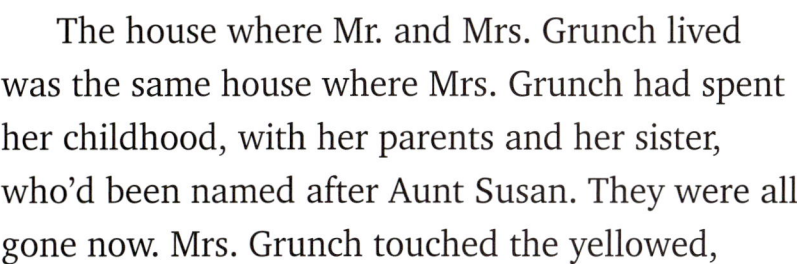

The house where Mr. and Mrs. Grunch lived was the same house where Mrs. Grunch had spent her childhood, with her parents and her sister, who'd been named after Aunt Susan. They were all gone now. Mrs. Grunch touched the yellowed, fragile, brittle envelopes gently. Memories erupted, filling her with joy and sadness, all at the same time. She selected an envelope and opened it.

"My goodness," she remarked, her eyes moist. "I had forgotten what beautiful handwriting Aunt Frances had. In those days, stylish writing was an art, and Frances admired art. Nobody typed then." Silence filled the dank attic room and she became engrossed in Frances' letter.

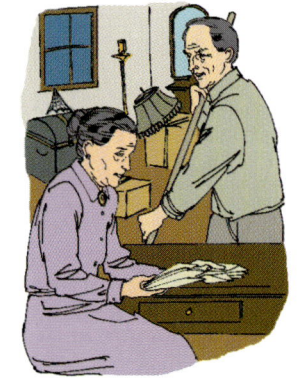

"Come on, Myra," Mr. Grunch interrupted. "We need a system here. You can't keep stopping and investigating everything. We're supposed to be getting rid of all this old stuff!"

The old-fashioned stationery featured an angel playing a lyre at the top. Myra Grunch's aunt, Frances Hyde, had used this stationery to correspond with her sister, Sydney Hyde White, for a period of twelve years, after Frances had gone to live in California. For those 12 years, from 1920 to 1932, Myra's mother, Sydney, corresponded regularly with Frances—mostly about the daily events in Jasper. Some of her letters were there too! The letters, Myra discovered, were a window on the past. Not just the events of the past, but the feelings, the very breath of those who once occupied this house.

Myra could remember Aunt Frances Hyde. A great beauty, Frances had gone to California in hopes of becoming a film star. After 12 years in Hollywood and several minor film roles (in early B movies nobody ever saw), Frances Hyde had been involved in a tragic, fatal accident and died in 1932. She was brought back home to Jasper for burial, and her belongings were stored in the attic of her childhood home. Myra recalled that Frances had been buried in the then-new cemetery, near the church that housed the crypts of her other ancestors.

"Myra. Myra!" Walter Grunch was exasperated. "Are you going to get with the system, or are you going to sit here and read a bunch of old letters? Hmm. Well, then, I'm going to take a break. I'm going downstairs. I'll bring you some iced tea. Then let's get back to it, old girl. The movers will be here day after tomorrow!"

Myra didn't answer. She sat among the pile of old letters, engrossed in the past. Walter edged gingerly down the rickety old attic steps, shaking his head. He knew better than to try to interrupt Myra when she was so engrossed. Nothing would break her train of thought.

Myra's legs felt cramped. She picked up the pile of old magazines from the seat of her grandmother's oak rocker, making a place to sit down. Her mother had rocked her in this chair. Granny Dolen had rocked Myra's mother in this very same rocker. She could almost feel their presence in the well-worn wood. So much life had been lived in this house—her family's history—everything that had made her Myra. She sat gingerly on the creaky old rocker and returned to one of Frances' letters. It was interesting, reading about those old movies, some made even before talkies. Didn't she recall hearing that Frances had actually known Charlie Chaplin, Cecil B. DeMille, and William Randolph Hearst?

"We're beginning work on a film called *The Myth of the Crystal Cypress*," Frances had written. "I'm told it's based on a legend from back East. Do you remember when we were girls and we heard about a magic old tree they called the crystal cypress? It was someplace along the sea, someplace not far from where they've built the new Long Ridge Lodge."

Myra smiled. Today, most people thought of the Lodge as one of the town's earliest public buildings. She heard Walter's footsteps on the creaky old stairs, and put the letter down to share a few minutes and a refreshing glass of iced tea with this man who had been her husband for so many years.

"Here you go," said Walter, her glass of tea in hand. Myra Grunch knew that lots of people thought her husband was a grouchy old man. But she knew differently. Myra knew that Walter's hearing was so poor that he often didn't fully understand what people were saying. Worse, sometimes he didn't hear at all.

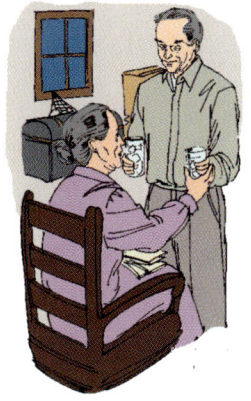

When he didn't respond, sometimes people thought him disagreeable. It was they who didn't understand. This man was kind and generous. Although they had had disagreements over the years, Myra had never regretted the day she had married Walter Grunch.

"This house is turning into a hydraulic disaster!" Walter complained. "First, the outdoor hydrant rusts out, and now, the plumbing under the kitchen sink is leaking. I turned the water off. We'll have to use the bathroom faucets until I can get a repairman in here."

Myra hung on to his words. She considered every syllable he spoke an unpolished gem. When she had been in the hospital, she recalled, Walter had been at her side every moment. She would never forget him whispering to her, "Myra, old girl, I can't do without you. You're all I have. I have loved you more than life itself. Please don't leave me. I love you, Myra."

It was Walter's daily encouragement that eventually brought Myra back and gave her the will to live, to do the exercises the doctors had insisted on, to change her diet. Myra was much better now, and she intended to go right on doing exactly what the doctors told her. Yes, Myra intended to live as many more years with Walter Grunch as life and time would permit.

"Walter," she sighed, "Do you remember when we were kids, hearing about a legend of a cypress tree at the edge of the sea? The crystal cypress?

"Supposedly," Myra continued, "it had some kind of magic. It had something to do with the people who first settled here in the early 1700s. Do you remember?"

"What in the world brought that to mind?" inquired Walter. Myra could tell that he was reading her lips. She wished that he would go to get a new hearing aid, one that could clear up muddled speech. But she knew he was worried about the bills.

"Well," Myra revealed, "it's this letter from my Aunt Frances—you remember, she's the one they called the free spirit—the one who went out West to be in the movies. It's a letter to my mother, from 1928.

"In this letter, Frances talks about a film called *The Myth of the Crystal Cypress*. She asks my mother if the myth's not the same one that started right here in Jasper, back in the early 1700s."

"Funny you should mention that," Walter replied, taking a sip of his tea. "Just yesterday, I was down at the dock talking to Ted. He was telling me that once back in '59, some gypsies came through, asking questions about that old crystal cypress story. I guess they went to ask Ted because somebody told them he was the only one around who knew about the legend."

"So what did Ted tell you?" inquired Myra.

"Hmm. Said they were only here a few hours, and then drove on. Didn't know what happened to them," Walter responded.

"Not about the gypsies, Walter! About the crystal cypress!" Myra was trying hard to recall something she once knew as a child, but had since forgotten.

"Oh, that. Well, Ted seemed to think that there had actually been a cypress tree. Had something about it that the old folk revered. Maybe there *was* a tree they called the crystal cypress. May still be there, for all I know."

"Listen, Walter." Myra began reading the letter. She felt like she was shouting, but she wanted him to hear the words Aunt Frances had written to her mother those long years ago. "Sydney, what was it that gave us the courage (or gall!) to take Uncle

William's new car on that rutty old dirt path down to the sea in search of the crystal cypress? Do you remember the day? I remember it as if it were yesterday. We didn't even know

how to drive! It was the summer of 1913."

Frances had continued in her letter, "At first, we didn't see the cypress trees at all! Just sand and shore, rocks and a few shrubs. A few years earlier, they had built the first yacht club right at the edge of that road. Before the new club was built at the dock. Remember?"

Myra set her glasses on top of the magazine pile. "So what do you think of that, Walter! Evidently the crystal cypress was somewhere near the first yacht club. Later, you know, that's where they built Long Ridge Lodge. Can't you just see them? Mama and Frances, a couple of girls, taking old Uncle William's car!"

"By golly, that's it!" blurted Walter, standing with a start. "Come on, old girl. We're going for a ride!"

"What?" Myra was astounded by her husband, who was usually the conservative in the family. "I thought we had to finish cleaning out the attic!"

"The attic will still be here when we get back. We're going to take a look at the crystal cypress while the sun's still high." Myra Grunch had never seen Walter more excited.

As their trusty old car neared the interstate's Long Ridge Road exit, Walter began singing, "Ride away with me, Lucille, while I hold on to the wheel."

"You'd better not be riding with any Lucille," teased Myra, "or she'll have me to deal with!" The two had not had such a lighthearted drive in longer than they cared to remember.

As he pulled into the parking lot of the Lodge, Walter pointed toward its northeast corner. "Look up there, Myra. See the top branches of the biggest tree on the side of the Lodge? See how the leaves look like woven diamonds? That's it. That's the crystal cypress!"

"Walter, that's ridiculous," his wife admonished. "How could you know such a thing? There might not even be any such cypress!"

"There's a cypress, all right," he said. "And that's it. Something in that letter from Frances brought it all back to mind." Walter helped Myra out of the car.

"Do you think you can walk that far?" he asked.

"Good heaven, Walter!" Myra chided him. "Of course I can walk that far. It's just whether I want to. What in the world is going on? What was in the letter? What is it you remembered? Tell me!"

"All in good time," he said, gallantly taking her arm and teasing her with his funny little bow. The two set off for the tree.

On the side porch of the Lodge sat hand-hewn tables and chairs under droning overhead fans. A waiter came out and asked if they'd like something to eat or drink. "My good man," Mr. Grunch told him. "In an hour or so, I want you to lay out the most elegant dinner you have to serve. I have a date with my best girl, and I will have nothing but the best for her. Nothing but the best!"

The young man nodded and replied, "Certainly, sir." He went back through the veranda doors, shaking his head and mumbling about crazy old coots.

"So what in the world is this about, Walter? I've waited long enough!" Myra Grunch was usually patient, but she couldn't wait.

"Hold your horses, old girl. Hold your horses. Do you see how the roots of this cypress tree grow down and then reemerge above the ground? Do you see how the pattern extends into the woods, back behind the Lodge?" Walter had a twinkle in his eye.

"I see. I see. So what in the world does that have to do with the myth?" Myra had lost her patience. "I'm getting chilly, Walter. The clouds have hidden the sun and it's getting cool out. What in the world are you trying to prove?"

"I just happen to have your favorite blue sweater in the back seat of the car," replied her husband. "I'll be right back!"

"Walter! Walter!" she shouted after him. "If I didn't know better, I'd think you were daft!" Now Myra was thinking her husband *was* a crazy old coot.

He was almost skipping from the parking lot toward the Lodge. "For heaven's sake, Walter. You'll fall and hurt yourself. What in the world is wrong with you?"

"Wrong? What's wrong? Nothing's wrong, old girl. Nothing. I just happen to have remembered what it was about this tree. And I wanted to share it with my best girl. Now put on your sweater and follow me."

"I will, but I don't know why," muttered Myra. Her husband was conservative. An accountant. He was smart. He didn't act foolish or do things on a whim. Everything he did had a reason. "What in the world is he thinking?" his wife wondered silently. Walter took her hand, cautiously leading Myra into the woods.

"Look up. Just look straight up among the very top branches," he said firmly.

The sun had peeked back out from behind the clouds. "Good heavens, Walter. Look how that gleams! I've never seen such a thing. What causes that? It looks like the sun is reflecting off crystals in the top branches of this tree!"

"Of course, old girl. Of course. That's why the old folk called it the crystal cypress. When the first settlers arrived in this county in the early 1700s, they discovered this tree and decided that it was magic. The sun still reflects off those branches in the same way it did then. When Frances wrote about driving down that old dirt path to get here, I remembered something. When I was a small boy, I once came down here with my father. He told me about how the crystal cypress got its name. He said that throughout history, people believed the cypress had protected Jasper from all kinds of disasters that hit other places. That's why they didn't chop it down when they built the Lodge. Instead, they just built right around it!"

"But what about the magic? What about the myth?" Myra still didn't understand. "Why was it all forgotten?"

"There's no magic, Myra. You know that. What protected our ancestors was their faith in themselves. Truth is, the magic's in the universe. People just keep on going, one generation after another, living, loving, doing their best. Life itself. That's the magic." Under the crystal cypress, Walter Grunch kissed his best girl.

Vocabulary Expansion

Describe and define these words and phrases:

longer than they cared to remember
efficiency apartment
crystal ball
band of gypsies
fatal accident
minor film roles
sat gingerly
train of thought
reading her lips
window on the past
an unpolished gem
muddled speech
funny little bow
crazy old coot

there's no magic
ancestors
named after
talkies
cypress tree
B movies
back East
out West
my best girl
daft
free spirit
legends

William Randolph Hearst
Charlie Chaplin
Cecil B. DeMille
Al Jolsen
hydraulic disaster
hold your horses
get back to it
rambling Victorian house
get with the system
worried about the bills
conservative in the family
their faith in themselves
the magic's in the universe

Language Expansion Activities

1. Draw a time line. Then list these events in sequential order:
   - Mrs. Grunch finds her Aunt Frances' letters.
   - Gypsies drive through town, stopping to ask about the cypress.
   - Mrs. Grunch has a heart attack and is hospitalized.
   - Frances Hyde moves to California to seek a career in films.
   - Aunt Susan puts the letters in the attic.
   - Preparing to move, Mr. and Mrs. Grunch pack their attic.
   - Sisters Frances and Sydney Hyde take Uncle William's car.
   - Doctors instruct the Grunches to move to an efficiency apartment.
   - Frances Hyde is involved in a tragic accident.
   - Mrs. Grunch's mother dies.
   - Mr. and Mrs. Grunch drive out to Long Ridge Lodge.

2. Ask a family member to tell you everything he or she can remember about the people in your family and about your ancestors. Then, write about your family in story form. If nothing is known about your family, create a family you'd like to have and write a fictional report.

Language Expansion Questions

1. Why were Mr. and Mrs. Grunch moving?

2. What clue had Frances Hyde's letter contained? Explain how the letter helped Mr. Grunch remember about the crystal cypress myth.

3. What had the gypsy leader told Ted when he drove through town back in 1959? Discuss what you know about gypsy culture.

4. Myra Grunch's Aunt, Frances Hyde, was described as a free spirit. What do you think that means? Do you know about any ancestors in your own family who were free spirits? Learn about them and share their lives with your group.

5. Describe the thoughts that Myra Grunch had while she was sitting in her attic, sorting through piles of things that had belonged to her family.

6. If you had been Myra's mother, how would you have felt about your sister going off to California to try to make it in the movies? Why would things have been different than they are today? Find somebody who remembers the early movies and ask him or her to tell you about them. Share the information with your group.

7. When the gypsies drove through, whom did they ask about the crystal cypress tree?

8. This book contains a story within a story. What are the two separate stories? How are they woven together? Explain why time, in a story within a story, can be confusing. Why is it interesting?

9. What do you think of Walter's explanation about the tree? After reading this story, how do you feel about Mr. and Mrs. Grunch?

10. Discuss Walter and Myra's relationship. Would you like to have that kind of relationship in a marriage? Why?

Unit 51
DIRT BIKE BOZO

UNIT 51

Phonology/Orthography Concepts

- Following are the conditions for **encoding** the phoneme /j/:
  - **Before a, o, or u,** /j/ is spelled **j**.
  - At the **beginning** of a word, **before e** or **i**, /j/ is spelled **j** or **g**.
  - In the **middle** of a word, before **e** or **i**, /j/ is spelled **g** (except in **ject**).
  - **After e**, /j/ is spelled **g**.
  - **After** short vowels in one-syllable words, /j/ is spelled **-dge**.

Vocabulary

age	generous	janitor	jog	page	*debt*
agent	gentle	jar	join	pajamas	*forward*
badge	germ	jeans	jump	plunge	
bridge	giant	jeep	just	project	
cage	gin	jelly	jut	range	
edge	ginger	Jen	large	register	
emerge	gist	jerk	ledge	reject	
emergency	grudge	jest	lodge	rejoice	
energetic	hinge	jiffy	logic	ridge	
fringe	huge	jig	magic	strange	
fudge	injury	Jill	margin	subject	
gem	interject	jingle	object	teenager	
general	jam	job	oblige	tragic	

DIRT BIKE BOZO

Story Summary:

Tom Vonert has his friends over to watch a dirt bike race on TV. His older brother, Bo, ridicules the boys for being impressed. Bo sets out to prove that *anybody* can be a dirt bike racing star. Bo finds out the hard way that he is wrong.

The boys sat on the edges of their seats, gathered around the family room TV in the Vonerts' house. "What a leap!" the sports announcer's voice boomed. "Jumping off the three meter ramp are dirt bike freestylers Jeffrey Jones and Eugene Bridge. These two champion freestylers are examples of what gives the Bicycle Motocross-Cross Freestyle event such an avid following!"

It was Saturday, and the six teenagers were supposed to be working on a collaborative science project. Instead, they had opted to watch the special all-sports channel dirt bike event.

"Check out that wheelie," shouted Sam Webster. "Gymnastics on a bike! I love this sport!"

"Man!" shrieked Nick Hopkins, splashing ginger ale all over his jeans. "Those guys can really cut it. Check out those four guys taking a sweeper around that turn at the berm. Whee-o! I can't believe they made it around."

"Tactics and technique," remarked Al Long, "that's what those bikers have in common. They race so close together, but did you ever notice that they don't actually touch? Physical contact is not allowed. You're only allowed to block a rider from behind."

Al was the intellectual of the group. He never got into a sport without knowing all the rules. And he really knew all about dirt biking. Al had had a dirt bike since he was six.

Next year they would begin their first year at Jasper High. They were looking forward to starting a dirt bike racing/freestyling team there.

"If you ask me," remarked Mat Miller, plunging into a generous pile of nachos, "I'd say that track had enough twists and turns in it to wind itself all the way around Jasper and back again."

"Right on," laughed Nando Rozas. He jumped up and mimicked another freestyler. "Check out this endo." Nando imitated a head-over-handlebars act, pretending to balance himself over the front wheel of an imaginary bicycle.

"You fool!" Nick teased. "You look like a nerd on a nose dive!"

They were roaring with laughter when Tom's brother, Bo, sauntered into the room.

"You juvenile rejects aren't watching that stupid dirt bike racing stuff, are you?" chided Bo.

The laughing stopped immediately. Everyone stared at the TV. No one liked Tom's older brother. The spirited group suddenly turned solemn.

"Why don't you mind your own business?" Tom muttered.

Tom always got angry and embarrassed when his brother Bo showed up. Bo, now 19, had just barely graduated from Jasper High last year. He still hadn't gotten a job. He hadn't taken any tests to get into college, and had shied away from trade school. He was drifting from part-time job to part-time job—when he could find one. He was known around town as a troublemaker and a general nuisance. Yet, for some reason, he had an annoying superior attitude toward his younger brother, Tom, and his friends.

"You bozos don't actually think that stuff is hard, do you?" Bo persisted.

"That *stuff*, as you call it," Al informed him, "is not something someone can just get on a bike and perform. Those riders have had years of training and experience. First of all, you have to learn how to control the bike," Al's voice revealed his irritation.

"Yeah," Sam joined in. The group of younger boys were united in their feelings about Bo. Sam supported Al, "You have to wear special safety equipment, like a lightweight helmet and padded pants. Or you're likely to get hurt."

"That's bunk," blurted Bo, grabbing some nachos from his brother's plate. Bo had a way of really getting to Tom's friends. "Anybody can do tricks like that," he insisted. "Why, I've seen four-year olds do better than those guys on TV!"

"I'd like to see you try it," challenged Nando. Nando would stand up to anybody. He had once saved a famous Mexican rancher from falling off a cliff in the Grand Canyon while he was on vacation with Nick's family. "I'll bet you can't ride as well as you think you can."

"There's nothing to it," responded Bo with a nasty smirk. "I'll get out my trusty old dirt bike and show all of you a trick or two."

The group fell silent again. The others shared knowing glances with each other, cognizant that Bo really couldn't competitively ride a bike. Mat smiled at Tom and then turned to Bo.

"How about some real competition?" Mat challenged Bo. "There's a dirt bike race over at the Long Ridge Lodge next Saturday. If you're so great, why don't you enter that competition and show everyone just what you can do?"

Bo hesitated for a second. It was just enough of a pause to give the others a chance to jump in.

"Yeah," Al challenged, "what about it, Bo?"

"He won't do it," Tom warned. "My brother is all mouth."

Bo considered Mat's challenge. He hadn't even been on his bike for more than three years. But he didn't want to look like a fool. Certainly not in front of his younger brother's friends.

At last Bo responded. "No problem. I'll show you and the rest of the jerks just how simple it really is. You're on!" Bo revelled at the thought of showing off in front of a crowd. He always loved being the center of attention.

"You're the jerk!" Tom shouted at his older brother. "Those pros will break your neck."

Bo leaned forward and stuck his face right in Tom's. It was his way of intimidating his younger brother. "We'll see, chump!"

Bo left without further word. The others went back to watching the race. But underneath it all, Tom was kind of worried about Bo. He was sure his brother had gone a little *too* far this time. But what could he do? If his brother wanted to be a jerk, let him. "It's going to take more than a magic potion for Bo to get out of this one without major injuries," Tom thought to himself.

    The next week, Bo kept busy practicing on his old dirt bike. He oiled it and replaced some of the rusty parts. He set up start/stop lines in his back yard, and he practiced slide stops and wheelies.

    Thursday after school, Bo called Tom out to the back yard to have him watch his "spectacular jumps." He did well, at first. But then he became foolhardy, landed wrong, and twisted his ankle.

    Seeing that Bo was just slightly hurt, Tom cautioned, "Bo, forget about the race on Saturday. It's only Tuesday and you're already hurt. Just think what might happen when you're racing with ten or twelve pro bikers. Face it, Bo, you just haven't got what it takes to be a dirt bike competitor."

    "Thanks for all your confidence and support, man," Bo shouted, rubbing his left ankle.

"You'll never learn, will you?" Tom muttered, shaking his head as he headed toward the back door.

"You're a loser," Bo shouted after him.

"Me!" Tom turned in disbelief. "You just don't see it, do you?" Tom shut the door and disappeared inside.

Bo reluctantly got up from the ground, continuing to massage his ankle. He stood up, but his leg was shaky. Was he a fool to take on such a challenge? He was determined to show that he could do it. He decided to give up for the day and go visit his Uncle Wally. Maybe he could offer Bo some advice.

Uncle Wally was Bo's only friend. Tom always said they had lots in common. Uncle Wally and his wife, Aunt Evanna, had lived with the Vonerts after Wally lost his job. Uncle Wally still didn't have a job. But it's hard to land a job when you lounge around on the couch watching TV all day.

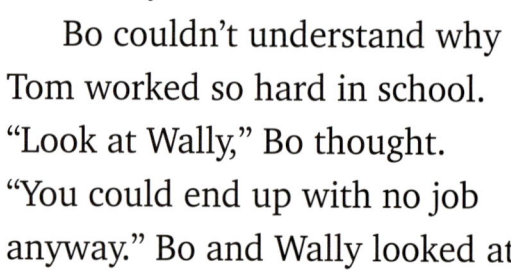

Bo couldn't understand why Tom worked so hard in school. "Look at Wally," Bo thought. "You could end up with no job anyway." Bo and Wally looked at the world in a negative way. There was no justice.

Bo trudged over to Wally's to have a talk with him about the competition.

"You're not actually going to enter that race, are you?" asked Wally after Bo told him his story.

"Why not?" Bo asked. "I'm not so bad."

"That dirt bike racing stuff you see on TV is for jerks," Uncle Wally commented as he popped open another can of soda. "Why risk it?"

"But, Wally," Bo said, "I've already taken on the challenge."

"There's your problem, Buddy," Uncle Wally maintained. "You've gone and shot your mouth off again. I'm not going to be able to get you out of this one."

"Like you've ever gotten me out of anything before," Bo shouted. "I'm out of here. You're the one who's got a big mouth."

"Fool kid," laughed Uncle Wally, as he heard the latch on the front door close.

Bo felt worse. But he was still determined not to quit. He was resolved to practice even harder. Even if it took

every hour for the next three days.

As the day of the race approached, everyone at school wanted to know how Bo was doing. Tom tried to avoid talking about Bo, but it was no use. Some of them even went over to Tom's after school one day to watch Bo from the back porch. They were amazed to see that he wasn't wearing a helmet or gloves. "I don't need all that safety equipment," Bo boasted. "That stuff is for kids!"

The boys laughed at him. Bo just got angrier.

The day of the race finally came. Bo went to register for the event early Saturday morning. Reality quickly started to close in. First, he was told he had to have safety equipment. Bo hadn't realized that in order to enter the race, he had to wear a helmet and gloves.

"You don't think you can actually ride in the race without the safety equipment?" the race official asked.

"Well," Bo muttered, "nobody told me about the equipment. Anyway, I'm not going to get hurt."

"Don't be so sure," the official warned him. "Racing is dangerous, especially for amateurs. Besides, it's the rules.

It doesn't take much sense to see that racing requires safety equipment," the official went on, his stern expression fixed on Bo.

Bo wanted to protest more. But the official saw it in his eyes and cut him off just as Bo was about to speak up, "Don't come back until you have the proper safety equipment. The padded pants and elbow guards are recommended, but optional," he continued. "And listen, kid, think carefully about whether or not you should participate here today. This is the real world here and everyone is treated equally. We've got only pro bikers registered. You *could* get hurt. Maybe even be hospitalized. And have you got insurance? This waiver you've just signed says that you are responsible for any injuries. Either you measure up to our standards or you don't race. Now, what is your answer? Are you in this race or out?"

"Aw, you're just trying to scare me. And it won't work!" Bo said. "I'll have the equipment before the race."

"I tried to warn you," the official said. "But have it your way."

Bo rushed off to the bike shop to get the safety gear. Suddenly Bo began to realize the severity of his foolhardy decision. He tried to fight the feeling that he was making a mistake. But it was no use.

He shrugged his shoulders and thought to himself, "I can do this. I just have to hang in there." But deep down he knew that he was making a mistake. Maybe even one of the biggest mistakes of his life.

The sun was shining when an eager, enthusiastic crowd began filling the bleachers. Colorful banners and flags adorned each row. Fans stood intently at the edge of the track, anticipating the gun and the first event.

"I almost didn't get away from my job at the bookstore," said Al, edging his way into an empty seat in the bleachers next to Tom and Sam. Al had been working at the bookstore on Saturdays to earn money to upgrade his computer. "Mr. Pasture has so much business now that he had to hire a lady full-time to keep up. So I was helping her with record keeping."

"You're not the last one here," reported Sam. "Nando and Nick are just coming up over the back of the bridge." With that, Sam let out a screeching whistle. Nick and Nando instantaneously responded with resounding whistles of their own.

"So," Al asked Tom, "is Bo ready for this?"

"As ready as he'll ever be, I guess," Tom shrugged.

"I tried all week to convince him not to enter," Tom remarked, "but he's the most thickheaded numskull I've ever met. Anyway, I guess I don't have to tell you guys."

"Is Mat coming?" Al wanted to know.

"He's over at the refreshment stand getting us some stuff to eat while we watch the race," laughed Tom nervously.

Tom was trying not to sound upset, but he had seen Bo practice. He knew that his brother was not prepared for today's events. Tom couldn't help but be worried. After all, regardless of how foolhardy and headstrong Bo could be, he was still his brother.

The Long Ridge dirt bike track started at the top of a steep hill. Several lanes were marked on it with chalk. A huge banner advertising the event's sponsor waved gently above the starting line. There were all kinds of jumps, bumps, and turns to negotiate before the finishing straight. The crowd waited anxiously for the starter's gun. Tom could see Bo in the third lane from the left.

Just this morning, Bo had bragged about how he was going to muscle his way through the event. But he didn't look like he was about to muscle his way through anything right now. Tom silently wished his brother luck.

"Geez," Mat shouted out from beneath the bleachers, "somebody come down here and help me!"

"The galloping gastronome has done it again," laughed Nick. "Come on, Nando, let's go give him a hand."

By the time they got to their seats, the starting gun had sounded, and the bikers were off. Bo got jostled at the starting line, but he managed to get going despite the setback. All the bikers were aiming for the hole shot, or leading position, on the first turn. You could tell Bo was riding as fast as he could, but the pro dirt bikers had already started to pass him. Just after rounding the first turn, Bo was bumped hard and he went down. To his credit, he got up and limped over to his bike. Bo was now at the back of the pack. A hairpin turn appeared just as the lead riders were getting ready to lap him.

It seemed like a dust storm in a stadium as the bikers rounded their second turn. The crowd roared as two bikers nearly crashed into the hay mounds lining the twisted track.

As the lead bikes began to draw away from the rest, Bo got bumped again. He flew off his bike, over the mounds of hay and into a nearby tree. His helmet was dented and he landed in a heap.

"Bo Vonert is down at the third turn. Medical personnel are on the scene," the voice over the loudspeaker announced. "We'll let you know how Bo is doing as soon as we have any information . . . ."

"Bo!" shouted Tom, leaping up from his seat and spilling soda all over the people surrounding him. Tom ran down on the track before officials had time to notice him.

"You'll have to get off the track, son," warned one official.

"But he's my brother!" shouted the distraught Tom.

Medical technicians immediately carried Bo off on a stretcher. He was barely coherent. Tom raced to his brother's side.

"Bo! Bo!" Tom cried out, "Can you hear me?"

"It's nothing," muttered a scarcely conscious Bo to his younger brother. "If it hadn't been for that stupid kid next to me this never would have happened."

"Foolish talk," claimed the medical technician attending Bo. "You could have been killed or paralyzed. Consider yourself lucky to have come out of this at all."

The comment sobered Bo. He acknowledged, "Maybe you were right, Tommy."

"Aw, you'll be OK now," comforted Tom.

Bo muttered, "Yeah, maybe."

Bo fell silent as the medical technician's injection started to take effect. Tom got in the ambulance with Bo and looked somberly out the rear window as his friends ran to the edge of the track.

Sirens wailed as the ambulance raced off toward the hospital.

"I'll call Mr. and Mrs. Vonert right away," yelled Al, racing toward the Lodge.

"Do you think Bo's OK?" Mat wondered.

"It looked like he was talking to Tom," said Sam. "I think that's a good sign."

"Let's get out of here," Nando suggested. "Suddenly this race doesn't interest me any more."

"Yeah," Nick agreed. "Let's go make some music. There's no thrill in watching people get banged up!"

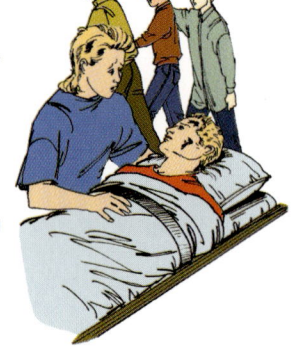

Vocabulary Expansion

Define and describe these words and phrases:

dirt bike racing	cut it	nerd on a nose dive
check it out	goon	thickheaded numskull
get into it	shy away from	talk so big
young rejects	freestyling	center of attention
bunk	all mouth	slide stops
jump in	go a little too far	shoot your mouth off
chump	show of support	measure up
wheelie	waver	hang in there
fool kid	foolhardy decision	muscle your way
fight the feeling	bozo	hairpin turn
makeshift	hole shot	
gastronome	edge of your seats	
	collaborative project	

Language Expansion Activities

1. Make a list of five to ten sports activities. For each sport, list the specific safety gear required. Why do some sports require more safety equipment than others? Compare your lists with those of others in your group. Then select one sport and write an essay about the importance of safety in that sport.

2. Design a dirt bike race track. Go to the library and check out books about the sport. Don't forget the hole shot, slide stops, and hairpin turns. Make a model, write a description of the track, and explain your project to the group.

Language Expansion Questions

1. What were Tom and his friends *supposed* to have been doing when they gathered at the Vonerts' house on Saturday? Why weren't they doing their project? Have you ever opted to do one thing when you were supposed to be doing another? Explain.

2. How did Bo get involved in dirt bike racing?

3. How did the story end? Do you think Bo got away with only superficial injuries, or was he really hurt?

4. Compare Bo's attitude before and after the race.

5. Why did the younger boys dislike Bo so much? Do you know anyone like Bo? Write a description of the person.

6. Why did Bo have a superior attitude? Do you think he was trying to hide his real personality? Why?

7. Identify the point at which Bo finally realized that he shouldn't have entered the race.

8. Create a new ending for the story. Assume that Bo won the race. How would that have changed things? Would the story have been more or less exciting?

9. Some stories have morals. Does this story have a moral? Explain your answer.

10. List some *good* qualities Bo possesses. Could Bo eventually turn his life around and start doing something useful? Do people ever really change? Have you ever changed? Do you know anyone who has? Discuss why people change.

Unit 52

CHANGES

UNIT 52
Phonology/Orthography Concepts
- The final **e** is silent under these conditions:
  - Following **cvc**
  - Following a soft /c/ or /g/
  - Following a single **u**, **v**, **s**, or **z** at the end of a word
  - In consonant + **-le**

Vocabulary

ablaze	attentive	confidence	exercise	plunge
above	attractive	conscience	existence	prize
abrasive	audible	consequence	extravagance	pursue
absolve	avenue	conserve	fragrance	range
abundance	axle	construe	freeze	refuse
acceptable	barbecue	continue	frieze	reprieve
acceptance	battle	contrastive	fringe	rescue
accessible	because	contrive	gentle	rose
accomplice	behave	cringe	give	rude
accrue	believe	curve	goose	sense
accuse	bereave	defective	grace	serve
achieve	binge	deference	grievance	singe
acquaintance	blouse	defiance	handle	single
active	breeze	degenerative	have	sneeze
adaptive	brilliance	deprave	hesitance	snooze
addictive	bronze	deprive	hindrance	squeeze
adhesive	browse	deserve	hinge	starve
admittance	bubble	despise	horse	statue
advertise	buckle	devise	imbue	strange
affective	cable	directive	immense	surge
affirmative	candle	dirge	issue	swerve
agile	captive	distinctive	jungle	table
alcove	carve	douse	kindle	thrive
alternative	challenge	eclipse	knave	tissue
amble	change	edifice	lounge	tweeze
ample	choice	elapse	lozenge	twelve
angle	circumstance	elegance	make	twinge
ankle	clearance	elusive	marble	value
announce	collective	emerge	nerve	valve
apple	commemorative	endurance	observe	virtue
apprentice	commerce	essence	orange	wheeze
argue	comparative	excellence	particle	
arrange	competence	excessive	payable	*half*
arrogance	comprehensive	exchange	phone	
article	conceive	executive	place	

CHANGES

Story Summary:

Sam Webster and his friends will be entering Jasper High School in the fall. Two of his old friends ask for Sam's help, and Sam is faced with making a difficult choice.

Sam Webster was leaving Tenth Street School for the last time. He'd filled his backpack with the last of the junk from his locker, and had unlocked his bike from the rack one last time. Everyone else was gone. Now, in the silent schoolyard, he struggled with the decision he had to make. Last week, Sam had realized that this would be a problem—a huge problem.

Sid North and Sam were good friends. When Sid had decided to run for Jasper High School student council next year, he had counted on Sam's support. Sid hadn't asked; he hadn't *needed* to ask, of course. When two people share a friendship like Sam and Sid's, they depend on each other's support. Asking isn't something you have to do. But now it looked as if Sam would have to say *no* to Sid.

Sam leaned against the top frame of the rusty bike rack, thinking to himself. "I have no choice. No matter what I do, somebody's going to be mad at me. I despise this. I'm between a rock and a hard place."

Last month, before she had told anybody else, Tam Turner spoke to Sam about running for student council. "I really want to do it, Sam," she confided. "It's just that I'm a little scared. I mean, what if nobody votes for me? I'd look like a fool. When my older brother and sister went to JHS, they were both on student council. So my mom and dad expect me to run. What should I do?"

Now Sam remembered how he had reassured Tam. "Plunge in. You can handle it!" he had told her. "Nobody else in our class has half your horse sense, Tam. You'd be great for student council."

"Big fool," Sam chastised himself. "Why didn't I keep my big mouth shut? Not me! I had to babble on. I had to volunteer to run Tam's campaign for her."

What was really bothering him was how to handle Sid. Sid was a gentle guy. He was always ready to help everybody else. Of all his friends, Sid was the one Sam had *always* been able to count on. Sometimes Al was too caught up in a computer project. Mat could be distracted by any offer that had anything to do with boats. Nick and Nando were involved with their band more than anything else. But it was different with Sid. Sam had always been able to count on Sid.

Sam stood staring at the ball field across the schoolyard. He remembered when they had first entered Tenth Street School as seventh graders. He remembered it like it was yesterday. For years, he and Sid and Al and Mat and Nick had played ball on that very field. Sam could almost hear their younger, carefree voices now, shouting and arguing gleefully. He smiled when he thought about Sid, a scrawny kid who had been no athlete. Last year, the coach had appointed Sid the team manager. Everybody loved Sid.

When had they stopped playing? When had they stopped being kids? When had life become so complicated? Now, because Sam had promised to help Tam Turner—weeks before Sid had talked to him—Sam had to tell Sid no.

Sam thought about how Sid had confided in him: "You know, Sam, everybody in our class respects you. If you back me for student council, it means I'll have a chance. I hadn't thought of running until we went over to the high school last week. Mr. Fell talked to me. He said he remembered me from the Martin Luther King speech contest. He told me I should run for student council because I

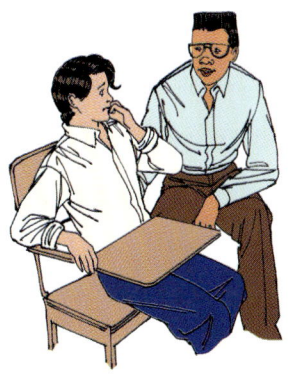

67

had leadership potential. First time anybody ever told me that. I never thought of myself as a leader. My mom was real proud when I told her. And suddenly, my little brother acts like I'm a hero. So now, like, I'm sort of obligated to run. Understand?"

Sam hopped on his bike and rode off. He wanted to stop thinking about it. Why hadn't he just told Sid the truth when he'd first asked for Sam's support? Now, a whole week had gone by, and Sid was coming to him every day with new ideas for his campaign.

Just this afternoon, Sid had asked if Sam thought his mom would let them use their basement during the summer to paint the posters. Campaign posters would cover the walls of JHS during the first two weeks of September—during the campaign for student council and class officers.

Not five minutes later, Tam had passed Sam's locker as he was cleaning it out. "Do you think we could get together next week to start planning the campaign, Sam? I'm so glad you offered to be my campaign manager. Now I'm not nearly as scared. I'll call you."

Sam decided to ride down by Mr. Pasture's. If Al was at work, he could talk it over with Al. Maybe they could come up with something. As he pulled up in front of the store, he saw Al inside. He and Mr. Pasture were both with customers.

Sam checked the traffic and sped back off toward the dock. He knew one thing for sure. He couldn't go home and talk to his parents about it. They'd argue with him and say he was crazy for promising the same thing to two people. They'd never understand. At Tenth Street, Sam turned right and headed toward the dock.

Sometimes when he had to think things over, the dock was the place he'd go. It was usually quiet by late afternoon. In the morning, charter boats and yachts headed out, and fishermen brought in their catch for the market. But by late afternoon, it was quiet. The shops would be closed; the place would be empty.

At the water's edge, an evening breeze stroked his face. In early June, it still cooled off by evening. Next month at this time, everybody would be sweltering in July's heat.

For some reason, Sam's thoughts turned to an old teacher, Miss Pitt, who had taught him in the sixth grade. He thought of the time Nick had hidden all her map pins, hoping Miss Pitt wouldn't call on him to identify countries in social studies class. Sam couldn't help laughing out loud. That was the year they'd had their class picnic in the rain. The year Scott moved to Louisiana and Nando moved to Jasper. Now Pat was moving to Wisconsin. Nothing would ever be the same again. Sam's eyes clouded over and his cheek felt wet. What he'd give to have those days back again! Now, everybody was always talking about driver's licenses and dates. Why did everything have to change? Why couldn't they just be kids a little longer?

"Sam? Sam! Boy, were you ever in another  world! I rode down here to get my dad's spare keys out of the store. He always forgets his keys. So what are you doing sitting down here by yourself? It's 6:00, man. Aren't you eating tonight?" It was his old buddy, Mat. His dear old buddy.

"Mat! Sit down. I thought your dad had started letting you drive from your house to the Fish Shack. Where's your wheels, man?" Sam was glad for the company. Mat hadn't changed. Mat would never change.

"Yeah. Well, I waxed his hatchback after school. I didn't want to get it dirty, so I just rode my bike down here to get Dad's spare keys. I've got a date with Molly tonight. You know. The 'Welcome New Students' dance at JHS?"

"You mean you're driving your dad's car tonight? You're taking Molly Manchester to the dance? I thought we'd just go together. Just the guys. I guess I'll call Al when I get home and see if he wants to go with me."

"Al and his date are going with us, Sam. He finally asked Kim this afternoon. You know Al. Finally got up enough nerve to ask a girl. I think he was shocked when Kim said yes!" Mat got back on his bike and warned, "Don't sit here too long, buddy. See you tonight!" With that, he was headed for home.

"Why didn't anybody tell me about these plans?" Sam wondered. He was feeling left out. In the old days, every time the guys had gone somewhere, they had gone together. Just guys. Tonight, Mat and Al weren't going with the guys. They were going with girls. And Mat was driving his dad's car.

Sam felt an unfamiliar emptiness—almost a feeling of pain. He rose slowly, and walked his bike up toward the hill. It was time to get home. He had never felt like this before. A deep sadness overwhelmed him, a kind of helpless, hopeless feeling.

After dinner, Sam's mother asked, "What time are you going? Are you supposed to get dressed up or is this the kind of thing where everybody wears jeans?"

"Just leave me alone, Mom!" he shouted. "I don't need my mother to tell me what to wear or what time to go. I'm in high school now. So just chill out!" Slamming the door of his room, Sam felt worse than ever. In the kitchen, his mother was left wearing a strange, wounded expression.

The phone in his room rang several times, but he ignored it. Finally, it stopped. Then, his mom was banging on his door, yelling that Sid was on the phone.

Sam tried to sound upbeat. "Yo. Sid. What's goin' on? You got anything on for tonight?"

"Aren't we going to the dance? I mean, like it's our first high school dance." Sid was hot to go. He couldn't dance any better than he could play ball. But then, Sam couldn't dance, either.

It hadn't taken Sid long to figure out that Sam was in a dark mood. Mostly, Sam was the guy who was always up. He didn't sit around griping. Sid realized that something had happened, but he didn't know what. He decided to leave Sam alone until he wanted to talk about it.

Inside, there were streamers and balloons and decorations all over the place. There was a live band, not just records like they'd had at dances in junior high. The lights were dim, and lots of people were dancing. Sid had been as surprised as Sam that Mat and Al had dates for the dance. But when they walked in, Sam and Sid were shocked.

Pat Marks was dancing with an older guy, a guy everyone knew. A senior. A basketball star. Sam knew how Sid felt. He'd always thought that when they got a little older, Pat would be his girl. It had been painful to learn that Pat was moving away, but to have to stand there and watch her dancing with this older guy—it was agonizing for Sid.

"Why didn't I ask Pat myself? What's wrong with me, Sam?" Sid felt regret and loss.

"There's nothing wrong with you, man. Nothing. It's everybody else. They're all changing. Everybody wants to be something different. Why does everybody have to change? Why can't it just be the same as it always was?" Sid had never seen his friend like this. It wasn't that Sam was mad. It was something different. Like Sam was really depressed about something.

"OK, man," Sid suggested. "Let's lose this place. I'd starve if I had to eat the stuff they serve at these things. Wanna go out and get a hamburger? Fries? Nothing's going down here. Nothing at all."

Sam was grateful. For a brief moment, as he and Sid left the dance, his spirits lifted. But walking down the dimly-lit street together, Sam remembered that he had something to tell Sid, something that would upset Sid. Once more, emptiness surged through him.

"Sam, about the campaign . . . ." Sid broached the subject, unsure of whether Sam wanted to talk about anything.

"I'm really tired of your campaign," Sam blurted. "You and Tam and everybody else. What about me? Nobody cares about how I feel. Everybody's so worried about themselves!" Sid North had never witnessed his friend Sam flying off the handle. Certainly not this way. Usually agreeable, Sam was the one who tried to patch things up between other people.

For the next five minutes, they walked in silence. The moon was full tonight, and its light filtered down through the leaves in the trees. People were sitting outdoors on their porches. It was only 9:30, and on this early June night, the promise of summer whispered from everywhere.

"Listen, Sam," Sid began again. "You really don't have to do anything with this campaign stuff. Honest. I had just thought about doing something different, and I thought you might tell me what you think about it."

Immediately, Sam felt like a louse. This was Sid. Sid, who had always been there when he needed him. Sid didn't deserve his dark mood. "Sorry, Sid. I don't know what's wrong with me. Let's talk about the campaign. I needed to talk to you about it anyway." Just ahead on the next corner, they could see the red neon lights of the diner.

"Well, Kim and Al were talking after science class. She was telling him that Tam was running for student council. So I thought, 'Why have two friends running for the same thing? Maybe I'll run for class president.' Do you think I'd have a chance? I was just thinking, all of the rest of you guys are going to be playing some kind of sport. Everybody knows I won't make any team. So I thought maybe I'd try for class president. I probably won't win, but . . . . You think it's a dumb idea, don't you, Sam?" Sid felt more than a little embarrassed.

"Sid North, I think it's a genius idea. An absolute brainstorm. I think we'll run the best  campaign in the country, and you, my man, will win. Absolutely." For the first time in several hours, Sam felt like things might turn out OK. They just might. "Sid, old buddy. I'm treating tonight. The hamburgers are on me!"

"It's a good thing, since you owe me from the last two times, Mr. Generosity!" Sid slapped Sam on the back, and the two raced into the diner. Since they had all been ten years old, they had always raced to see who would be first to scoot into the worn, green leather booths near the front. It was a kind of ritual. Now, they didn't remember *why* they did it. They just did.

The diner always smelled the same. Sizzling onions, a pungent cleanser they used on the counters, and other odors combined, creating its distinct aroma.

Familiar and comfortable, the diner was the place they could talk about anything. Sam began, "Sid, there's something I wanted to tell you about this campaign . . . ."

"Hey, you guys! Wanna come back here and sit with us?" interrupted Tam Turner, calling from a booth across the room. "We're just sitting here being miserable!" She was sitting with Nick and Nando.

Sid got up, so Sam followed. The two scooted into the booth with their three friends. "So what are you three so miserable about?" Sid asked.

"Aw, Tam's just thinking about the dance. She wanted to go, but she was too ugly. Her friends had dates." Nick Hopkins teased Tam, rubbing the top of her head with his fist. "Don't know what we're gonna do with this girl. May as well give her away."

"What about you, Mr. Cool Hopkins? You know you wanted to go with Molly, but you waited until the last minute and she had already told Mat yes."

Tam wasn't exactly kidding. The tone of her voice said that she was feeling a little bit fiery.

"Come on, you two. Cut it out. If you'd really wanted to go, you'd have gone." Ever the peacemaker, Sam couldn't stand to hear his friends arguing.

"OK, OK," agreed Tam. "So let's talk about my campaign. Did you guys know I'm going to run for JHS student council? Sam talked me into it. He volunteered to be my campaign manager."

Sam wanted to crawl under the booth. Sid looked at him with a pained expression. "When did this happen, old buddy?" You could tell Sid was hurt. Sid didn't get mad like a lot of guys. He would just be hurt, and Sam couldn't stand that.

"I was just getting ready to explain when Tam called us over here a minute ago," Sam began. "See, I had offered . . . when, Tam? . . . about a month ago . . . to be her campaign manager. Then when you came to me last week . . . it's just that you were so excited and I couldn't find the words to tell you."

"So can you still manage my campaign for class president?" Sid asked. No grudges. That was Sid.

"You're running for president? Sid, what a great idea!" Tam was gleeful. "Maybe a bunch of us could run on a slate. Sam could run the whole campaign! We could have so much fun this summer, doing posters and making up raps and stuff. By the time school starts, we could have everything ready! Sam, what do you think?"

Nick was doubtful. "Man, everybody knows Sam's gonna be captain of the JV football team. How's he supposed to be able to do all this election stuff?"

"But we don't start practice 'til the last week of August," retorted Sam. "By then, we can have it all finished! We'll use my basement. Mom said no problem. We're on. Let's plan our slate. This will be the best tenth grade class JHS has ever seen!"

Vocabulary Expansion

Describe and define these words and phrases:

horse sense	leadership potential	he was no athlete
brainstorm	wounded expression	eyes clouded over
chill out	a guy who is always up	got up enough nerve
dark mood	felt a surge of regret	nothing's going down
live band	his spirits lifted	captain of the JV team
slate	broached the subject	crawl under the booth
always up	fly off the handle	promise of summer
patch things up	felt like a louse	wasn't exactly kidding
distinct aroma	make up raps	feeling a little fiery
tone of voice	look like a fool	you can handle it
peacemaker	campaign manager	

Language Expansion Activities

1. Select a candidate who is running for a local, state, or national office. Decide how you would run that person's campaign. Write a speech for the candidate to make to a group of voters. Then, create a campaign logo and a "tag line" to be used throughout the campaign. When you have finished, send your work to the person. Share the person's response with your group.

2. Write a letter to Sam Webster. Try to help him understand the feelings that have been bothering him. Give him some advice about what he should do. Consider his friends, his parents, his school activities, and his life in general. Make sure that your advice is both realistic and helpful.

Language Expansion Questions

1. Sam had to make a choice between two friends. Discuss his quandary. Was there an obviously right or wrong choice? If you had been Sam, would you have handled it differently?

2. Discuss the title of this story. Is it appropriate? Why?

3. Something else was bothering Sam. It was much larger than the choice between supporting Tam or Sid. What was it? Explain why you think it affected Sam the way it did.

4. What kind of person is Sid North? Discuss his qualities, based on what you've read about him. Do you have any friends like Sid?

5. Tam and Sid both expressed concern about running for office. Both were afraid of looking foolish. Why did they feel the way they did? If you were their friend, how would you advise them?

6. Who had first encouraged Sid to run for office? Why? Describe how Sid's mother felt when he told her about his decision. What will she say when she learns her son is running for class president?

7. Discuss Sam's outburst when his mother asked what he was wearing to the dance.

8. When Sid called Sam *"Mr. Generosity,"* he was being sarcastic. What is sarcasm? When is sarcasm funny? When is it rude? In this case, was Sid's sarcasm funny or rude?

9. Explain why Sam felt such a deep sadness, *"a kind of helpless, hopeless feeling."* A few hours later, he was back to his old self. Has this ever happened to you? Explain the situation.

10. A universal theme is a basic truth about people everywhere, throughout time. Decide what this story's theme is. Is it universal? Discuss ways that Sam's experiences are similar to those of people in other places, in other times.

Unit 53
EVERY ENDING IS A NEW BEGINNING

UNIT 53

Phonology/Orthography Concepts

Encoding **long vowel** phonemes: /a/, /e/, /i/, /o/, /u/

- Orthography/phonology—graphemes/phonograms: **long** /a/:
  - The grapheme **a** represents long /a/: 1) at the end of an open syllable; and 2) in c **a** c followed by silent **e**.
  - The following phonograms also represent long /a/: **ay**, **ai**, and **eigh**.
- Orthography/phonology—graphemes/phonograms: **long** /e/:
  - The grapheme **e** represents long /e/: 1) at the end of an open syllable; and 2) when c **e** c is followed by silent **e**.
  - The following phonograms also represent long /e/: 1) **ee**, **ea**, **ie**, and 2) at the end of a word, **-y** or **-ey**.
- Orthography/phonology—graphemes/phonograms: **long** /i/:
  - Long /i/ is represented by the grapheme **i**: 1) at the end of an open syllable; 2) in c **i** c followed by silent **e**; and 3) when **i** is the first letter of a word's first syllable.
  - Long /i/ is represented by the grapheme **y**: 1) when **y** is preceded by a consonant or consonant blend; and 2) at the end of an open syllable.
  - Long /i/ is represented by the phonogram **ie** when a one-syllable word is an open syllable.
  - Long /i/ is represented by the phonogram **igh**: 1) when a one-syllable word is open; and 2) when **-igh** + **t** ends a word.
- Orthography/phonology—graphemes/phonograms: **long** /o/:
  - The grapheme **o** represents long /o/: 1) at the end of an open syllable; 2) when c **o** c is followed by silent **e**; and 3) when **o** is the first letter of a word's first syllable.
  - The phonogram **oa** represents long /o/ in c **oa** c words.
  - The phonogram **oe** represents long /o/ after an open syllable.
  - The phonogram **ow** represents long /o/ after an open syllable or in a single-syllable word.
- Orthography/phonology—graphemes/phonograms: **long** /u/:
  - The grapheme **u** represents long /u/: 1) at the end of an open syllable; 2) when c**u**c is followed by silent **e**; and 3) when **u** is the first letter of a word's first syllable.

Vocabulary

cube	humid	nude	rural	ukelele	universe	*bouquet*
cuter	humor	pupil	tuba	unicycle	usable	*butcher*
dude	lute	rebuke	tube	uniform	utensils	*promise*
duke	mucus	ruins	tulip	union	utility	*roll*
fumes	mused	rules	tuna	unique	utilize	*swan*
fuse	music	rumor	tutor	unite	utopia	*toll*
						young

EVERY ENDING IS A NEW BEGINNING

Story Summary:

Kim Chung's best friend, Pat Marks, is moving to Wisconsin to live on her grandmother's farm. Kim is upset because she is losing her best friend.

"My best friend is really moving today," Kim Chung sighed. "I just can't believe it. Oh, Mom!" she cried. "Pat just can't leave now."

"We've been over this a million times, sweetheart," Mrs. Chung said. "I know Pat has been your best friend for a long time, but you'll find a new one. Things change. Nothing lasts forever."

"You just don't understand," Kim complained.

"I understand more than you think I do. You know," Kim's mom went on, "Herbert Marks and I have been friends for much longer than you and Pat. In fact, we lived next door to each other before you and Pat were born. Jo Marks and I were best friends, too. Before she died you kids used to play together every day. Jo and I used to take turns watching you. I'm going to miss Herbert very much." Kim could see tears welling up in her mom's eyes.

"I'm sorry, Mom," Kim sighed, giving her mom a hug. "I guess I just wasn't thinking."

"You'll be lonely for a while, Kim," Mrs. Chung reassured her daughter. "You'll never forget Pat, but your pain and loss will ease with time. I promise."

Kim looked out the glass door into the back yard. The sun hadn't come out at all that day and the bleakness—so uncommon for a day in early summer—enveloped her. Her best friend was moving far away. She started to shiver, recalling things they had done together ever so many years ago. Kim had known Pat since early childhood. Pat's mom had still been alive then. They had played dress up in the Markses' attic at their old Raven Hill Road house. A trace of a smile found Kim's lips as she remembered the first time they had sung together. They used to make up songs in Pat's room. Then they would go downstairs in the dress up clothes and sing concerts for anyone who would listen. They had sung so off-kcy. Who would ever have thought Pat and Kim would later become members of the Long Ridge Glee Club?

Startled by the ringing of the phone, Kim raced to pick it up. Pat was on the other end.

"Hi, Kim," Pat began. "Can I come over?" she asked with a lump in her throat. "Dad said he'd bring me right before we left town. He wants to say good-bye to your mom, too."

"Sure," Kim agreed. "Please come. I just can't believe today's the day. When are you leaving?"

"We'll be there in about an hour," Pat said, an edge in her voice. "We have to wait for Trish. My sister is playing one last game of soccer with her team."

"OK. See you then." Kim sighed as she hung up the phone. Outside she could see the dogwood trees swaying in the thundering gusts. Their branches looked like open arms just waiting to encircle Kim.

Kim couldn't imagine what life would be like without Pat. Everything she had ever dreamed about or done had invariably involved Pat in one way or another. Kim remembered the secret hiding place she and Pat had used as kids—under the stairway next to the water heater in the basement. "I bet we're not the only kids who ever found this hiding place," Kim remembered Pat chiding.

But Kim had felt it was uniquely theirs. Back then. And what about the time they had started a health club in Pat's new basement? It was right before the cheerleading tryouts. They had really never worked out, actually. They used to meet there and eat cookies and ice cream. That was one thing they had never told Molly and Tam! Then there were the countless times they had played jokes on Pat's sister, Trish. Like the time Trish and her friend Sis were playing in the attic. Pretending to be frightful ghosts, Pat and Kim had nearly scared the younger girls to death.

"Who was that, dear?" called Kim's mom from the kitchen.

"It was Pat," Kim replied. "Pat and Trish and their dad are going to stop by before they take off."

"Well," said Mrs. Chung with a smile, "there's only one thing to do at a time like this."

"What?" asked Kim.

"Let's bake a cake," her mom suggested.

"Angel food?" questioned Kim.

"Angel food it is," agreed Mrs. Chung.

It was nearly two hours before the Markses pulled into the Chungs's driveway. Kim had never seen so much packed into one station wagon. The tires seemed to be squashed to their rims. The car was stuffed window to window with suitcases and boxes filled to the brim with family treasures. The rooftop canvas tarp bulged with a million bags and boxes.

"Holy Toledo!" Kim remarked to Mr. Marks. "How can you drive with all that stuff in the car?"

"It's not easy, Kim!" smiled Mr. Marks, shaking his head.

They all laughed. Mrs. Chung led them into the kitchen for some cake and milk.

Afterward, Kim and Pat went up to Kim's room. Pat had brought Kim a present. She wanted her to open it in private. "I can't even believe you bought me this!" Kim cried out as she opened her gift. It was a hardcover book on the great choirs of Europe.

"We're going to go there some day," Pat said with determination. "You and me. And we're going to really see the sights. And we'll hear some of the world's greatest choirs singing the best music ever written."

"I sure hope so," mused Kim. "I can't think of anyone I'd rather go with than you."

Pat's dad called upstairs, "It's time, sweetheart. We really have to go now."

As they walked out of the house, Mr. Marks looked up and noticed that it was getting very stormy out. "We need to reach the state line before dark," Mr. Marks said as he got into the station wagon. "And I'd like to avoid as much of this storm as possible."

Mrs. Chung gave Pat and Trish each a hug and kissed Mr. Marks on the cheek. "We'll miss you—everyone," Mrs. Chung said.

Teary-eyed, Kim hugged Pat. "And I'll really miss you," Kim whispered, a lump in her throat. Wisconsin seemed light years away.

"I'll write, too," Pat called out, lowering the window on the passenger side. "Promise."

Pat, Trish, and Mr. Marks drove away. When the station wagon disappeared, Kim's mom looked around and saw that Kim was gone, too. Mrs. Chung could just make out Kim's silhouette on her

bike as Kim rounded the corner at the end of the street. She thought about calling after her daughter, but then thought better of it. "Kim needs time to work out her feelings," she thought to herself.

The wind had really started to blow hard now. Mrs. Chung paused for a moment, glanced into the dark sky and, wrapping her arms around herself, scuttled into the house.

Three blocks away now, Kim was pedaling hard. She wasn't going any particular direction. She just needed to ride. Abruptly, she became very angry. "Why does *my* best friend have to move? Billions of people in the world and it has to be my best friend!" Kim was muttering aloud to herself as she journeyed along Swan Road. She was so deep in thought that she hadn't noticed that the wind was blowing fiercely. She pedaled harder and harder. A soft rain started to spray her face, but she hardly noticed it. Salty tears rained down her cheeks. She was quickly getting soaked.

Suddenly she found herself headed toward the dock. As she bounced onto the rickety timbers of Overlook Bridge, she lost control. Her bicycle spun into a piling. With a jerk, it overturned. Kim rolled to the ground hard and bounced to the edge of the bridge. She nearly landed in the churning white waters crashing below her.

Dazed, she got up slowly. She took stock of herself. She was unhurt for the most part, but couldn't put any weight on her left ankle. Her knee was badly skinned and quickly turning bright red. It really burned. She gazed down at her bike. The front tire rim was seriously bent. She tried to pick it up, and knew she couldn't ride it. The pelting rain began coming down in sheets. Kim realized that she needed to seek shelter. All of a sudden, she heard a strange voice behind her.

"Can I help you?" It was the handsomest young man Kim had ever seen. "Looks like you need to get that rim fixed and get inside. This storm won't be letting up any time soon. My Uncle Ted has a Shell Shop right across the street," he gestured. "Come with me over there and I'll see if I can fix it. Uncle Ted has every tool known to humankind!"

Startled, Kim was at a loss for words. She opened her mouth, but nothing came out. She composed herself, swallowed, and began, "You're Ted's nephew?"

"That's right," he answered. "My name's Pete Swan, and I'm visiting my Uncle Ted for the first time. My parents and I have been living in Portugal for the past ten years."

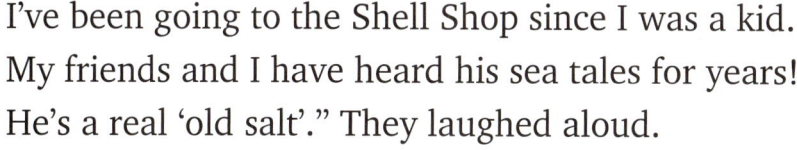

"Oh, wow!" Kim said, trying to behave casually, "I know Ted. I've been going to the Shell Shop since I was a kid. My friends and I have heard his sea tales for years! He's a real 'old salt'." They laughed aloud.

At that exact moment, a bolt of lightning exploded right behind them. Pete and Kim looked up at the instant it jolted Ted's Shell Shop. The whole dock was lit up like a baseball field during a night game. The explosion was so loud that Kim

and Pete had to cover their ears. Pieces of timber and shingles sprayed into the street in front of them. Heavy sheets of rain poured down on the dock.

Kim screamed louder than she ever knew she could and they both jumped back.

"Unbelievable!" Pete yelled. The shock was gone from his face in an instant and he rushed across the street to see if his Uncle Ted was OK. Store owners clad in rain gear began pouring out of the adjoining stores to inspect the damaged Shell Shop. Thunder continued to clap and the rain poured down, flooding the waterfront. Giant waves broke with a roar at the end of the dock.

Pete pulled what remained of the front door to the shop aside and shouted in, "Uncle Ted, are you all right?"

Kim followed behind, tottering on one leg. She was at Pete's heels as he entered cautiously. The other shop owners gathered behind them.

A feeling of relief overtook both Kim and Pete as they saw Ted hobbling across his floor. "It's OK, Pete," Ted shouted out, the sound of his voice comforting Pete for the moment. "Luckily I was in the basement when the bolt hit," he continued. "Lit up the place right pretty."

"What a mess!" gasped Kim, forgetting her own injuries for the moment.

Another store owner, Jen Wells, invited them all into her Pet Shop. Sirens screamed in the distance.

By the time the police and fire department arrived, Jen had gotten blankets and made coffee. Kim tried to call her mother, but the phone lines were down.

"I didn't even tell Mom I was going out for a ride," Kim said despondently.

"I'll talk to her for you," said Jen, giving Kim a hug. "Let's take a look at that leg of yours."

"Are you sure you're OK, Uncle Ted?" Pete asked. "Maybe we should ask the police to call an ambulance."

"No need, lad. I'm as OK as I'll ever be," Ted answered with his salty drawl. "But I wish I could say the same for my store." Ted walked to the window, resting heavily on his wooden leg. "No tellin' how much damage there'll be to that old shop. Oldest building at the dock," he said proudly. "Built her myself more than thirty-five years ago." Ted watched as the firefighters plodded through his shop, checking the rubble for any sign of fire.

"You never know," Jen said, tying a bandage onto Kim's aching knee. "I've seen other buildings where lightning has struck. Sometimes the damage wasn't as bad as it had appeared to be just after the original explosion."

"Sure, Jen," Ted replied, "but what about my stock? All those precious shells and trinkets. My life savings is tied up in there. Things are sure to be broken. Sure as we're standin' here talkin'."

"That may be true," Jen said. "But haven't you got some insurance? Remember that salesman who stopped by a couple of years ago and talked to both of us about increasing our policies? I know I did."

"Ya got a point there, Lassie," Ted said affectionately. "I do recall some high-powered salesman sellin' me a policy I thought I didn't need. I'll have to look that up in my files. Speakin' o' files!

I sure hope that lightnin' didn't crash into my file cabinet."

Ted and Jen kept talking about insurance policies. Kim and Pete sat near the puppy cages playing with a friendly litter of golden retrievers, getting to know each other.

Kim found that she was pouring her heart out to Pete. "It's funny," she thought to herself, "I never knew that you could talk to a boy this way." She found herself telling Pete all about her best friend leaving and how she felt so empty inside.

"I know what you mean," Pete explained. "I just had to leave my best friend in Lisbon. And that's a lot farther away than Wisconsin. I doubt we'll ever see each other again."

"I bet Pat and I won't see each other much either," Kim said. "Maybe her grandmother will let

me come visit for a few weeks in the summer. But it will never be the same."

"I know," agreed Pete. "Luis Selico and I always had so much in common. You'll probably think this is stupid or something, but Luis and I had just made the final cuts for the most prestigious choir in Portugal. We always loved singing, and it was the most difficult choir to get into."

"I don't think that's stupid at all," Kim announced. "It's one of the reasons Pat and I had so much in common. We both tried out for the Long Ridge Glee Club last year and made it. In fact, we are hoping to go to Europe someday. Pat gave me a book on the greatest choirs in Europe as a going away gift just today!"

"I'd love to browse through that myself," Pete declared. "I can't believe I found someone who loves music and singing on my very first day in town. What a fluke! Maybe the choir I tried out for is in your new book!"

Noticing that the storm had subsided significantly, Jen interrupted the two of them. "Listen, you two, the storm is passing. I told Ted that I'd drop him and Pete off at his house. I think it's time we all get out of here and go home."

"Oh, my bike!" Kim remembered with concern.

"I'm sure it's no worse than when we left it," Pete said. "I'll go get it for you."

"What's this about your bike, Lassie?" questioned Ted.

"I had an accident right before the storm hit. That's when I met Pete," Kim explained.

"Very convenient," Ted put in. He and Jen smiled at each other, knowing that Kim and Pete were fast becoming friends.

In a few minutes, they had all piled into Jen's van. They stopped at the bridge to pick up Kim's broken bike. The waves were still rough, but the whitecaps had subsided. The shrieking wind was silenced. And off in the distance sunlight broke through the clouds. Bright pink and orange rays poked through holes in the clouds.

When they arrived at Kim's house, Mrs. Chung rushed out to the van. She saw that Kim was inside and with a relieved look on her face, she said, "Kim, darling, I was so worried."

"I'm OK, Mom," Kim reassured her mother. "I've been with Ted and Jen."

"Kim tried to call you," Jen called out through the open window, "but the phone lines were down. Ted's shop was damaged, but no one was hurt.

"I bandaged Kim's knee," Jen went on. "No real harm, I suspect."

Mrs. Chung was glad to know that no one had been seriously hurt, and sympathized with Ted regarding his store.

"I'm so sorry, Ted," she said. "You know that if there's anything I can do . . . ."

Ted held up a hand as if to stop her. He said, "Thanks a lot, Mrs. C., but I've been thinkin' about that small shop just down the way. That place has been for sale for the past year. If I play my cards right I might just get a good deal on it with my insurance money!"

"Now you're talking!" Jen said enthusiastically. "Start thinking positively about a new beginning."

"Do you think I could drop by and see that book sometime?" Pete asked Kim as he took her bike out of the van. "I'd love to see if my choir is in it.

Maybe I can help fix your bike, too."

"Sure," replied Kim with delight. "Why don't you call me tomorrow? I'll be home all day."

Waving good-bye, Kim thought to herself, "A new beginning . . . ."

Vocabulary Expansion

Define and describe these words and phrases:

we've been over this	nothing lasts forever	things change
play group	playing dress up	off-key
feelings ease with time	secret hiding place	health club
cheerleading squad	rooftop canvas tarp	see the sights
state line	a lump in the throat	silhouette
rickety timber	lose control	let up
every tool known to man	old salt	night game
break with a roar	at his heels	empty inside
increase your policy	phone lines down	whitecaps

Language Expansion Activities

1. Pete had lived in Lisbon, Portugal. Write a report on Portugal. Include languages spoken, geographic layout, average temperatures, principal occupations, crops, exports, imports, industries, universities, chief ports, government, and a brief history of the country.

2. Pretend you are a local newspaper reporter. Write ten questions you could ask Ted concerning the lightning striking his Shell Shop. Conduct the interview with someone in your group. Then, report the incident as if you were a TV reporter. How are newspaper and TV reporting alike? How are they different?

Language Expansion Questions

1. Why was Kim so upset? When was the last time you were that upset? Explain.

2. What did Mrs. Chung mean when she said, *"Things change. Nothing lasts forever."*? Evaluate Mrs. Chung's wisdom.

3. Describe the Markses' station wagon right before they left for Wisconsin. Has your family's car ever been overloaded with luggage? Where were you headed? Recall the event.

4. Predict what would have happened if Pat and her family suddenly decided to stay in Jasper. Write the story.

5. Suppose you were Kim. What would you have done right after Pat moved away? What will happen to Pat and Kim?

6. At one point in the story, Kim got very angry. She felt like shouting at the world and ended up on the other end of a broken bike. Why did she feel the way she did? Were her feelings legitimate?

7. How were Ted and Kim each going to begin again? In what way are all endings really beginnings?

8. Mrs. Chung told her daughter, *"We've been over this a million times."* Has anyone ever said that to you? In what context?

9. Recall at least three times when the weather changed in the story to mirror Kim's feelings. Use this kind of imagery in your next story.

10. Select the character you would want to be—Kim or Pat—and tell why. Would you want to be moving to a new home or staying behind? Describe the particulars of each.

Unit 54

A WINNER NEVER QUITS

UNIT 54

Morphology/Orthography Concepts

- Adding suffixes to single-syllable words ending in consonants:
  - Double final consonant of **cvc** word to add suffixes beginning with a vowel.
  - Do not double the final consonant to add suffixes beginning with consonants.
  - Add suffixes to words ending in more than one consonant sound.

Vocabulary: One-Syllable Words Ending in Consonants + Suffixes

run+ner	hop+ping	red+dish	fit+test	drop+ped	bag+gage
quit+ter	sit+ting	thin+nish	big+gest	step+ped	stop+page
rap+per	chat+ting	hot+tish	hip+pest	tan+ned	lug+gage

bit+ten	fun+ny	pet+s	rich+ly	mist+ing	wax+es
rot+ten	mud+dy	sit+s	hard+ly	hard+ly	fix+es
sad+den	star+ry	pod+s	sad+ly	damp+en	box+es

- Adding suffixes to words ending in final silent **e**:
  - Drop final silent **e** to add suffixes beginning with vowels.
  - Do not drop final silent **-e** before adding suffixes beginning with consonants
  - Or when adding the suffixes **-able**, **-ous**, or **-ful**.
  - When adding the suffix **-ly** to words ending in **-le**, drop the **-le**.

Vocabulary: Words Ending in Final Silent -e + Suffixes

saf+er	lik+ing	styl+ish	saf+est	hik+ed	us+age	
fin+er	writ+ing	rav+ish	fin+est	rop+ed	mistak+en	
sur+er	handl+ing	mul+ish	sur+est	twinkl+ed	brok+en	

bon+y	hope+s	safe+ly	change+able	courage+ous	humb+ly	
tast+y	place+s	nice+ly	love+able	outrage+ous	simp+ly	
curv+y	fire+s	rare+ly	service+able	purpose+ful	gent+ly	

- Adding suffixes to words ending in **y**:
  - To add a suffix beginning with **e** (**-er**, **-est**, **-ed**) to words ending in consonant + **y**, change the **y** to **i**.
  - To add a suffix beginning with **i** (**-ing**, **-ish**) to words ending in consonant + **y**, retain the **y**.
  - To add a suffix (**-er**, **-ing**, **-ish**, **-est**, **-ed**, **-age**, **-able**) to words ending in vowel + **y**, retain the **y**.

Vocabulary: Words Ending in -y + Suffixes

dri+er	dri+est	tri+ed	carry+ing	baby+ish	play+er
fli+er	curli+est	fri+ed	apply+ing	puppy+ish	employ+er
cri+er	poki+est	suppli+ed	deny+ing		buy+er

stray+ing	boy+ish	gray+est	stray+ed	voy+age	pay+able
toy+ing	gray+ish	gay+est	toy+ed	dray+age	say+able
survey+ing		brey+ed	allay+ed	bon voy+age	buy+able

Vocabulary: Nonphonetic Words for Unit 54

cousin   cover   courage   enough   through   sugar   busy

A WINNER NEVER QUITS

Story Summary:

The new high school students are assigned to Mr. Fell's homeroom. This is Mr. Fell's last year of teaching. The students discover that the lessons he has to teach them are not always about world history.

Mr. Fell stood at the bank of windows of his second story classroom. He gazed down on the swarm of students waiting for the first bell's sharp ring. This would be his last year of teaching before retirement. He had memories of thousands of  students he had taught over his forty years, of the ways they had affected his life.

He hoped—no, he knew—he had affected their lives, too. He would never regret deciding to be a teacher. Lots of men he knew were paid better salaries than he, but he didn't know a single man whose chosen career had been more rewarding.

When the bell rang, his blue eyes twinkled. His homeroom students would be here soon. When students entered JHS, they were assigned to a homeroom teacher, and they stayed with that teacher until the end of their twelfth grade year. Mr. Fell's only regret was that he would not be here to see his new homeroom students graduate.

He looked at the roster of names of new students assigned to him, to see if he recognized any. These kids would be coming from Tenth Street School. Sid North. That was the kid who'd made that marvelous speech on Martin Luther King Day last year. Mr. Fell felt a pang. He was sorry he wouldn't be around to see that young man progress. He was sure that Sid North was going far. He noticed that there was a line through the name above Sid's: ~~Pat Marks~~. One of the school secretaries told him that she had moved.

Nick Hopkins. He'd met Nick. He remembered reading Nick's file. He was the kid teachers had thought was just slow, until they'd discovered he had a reading disability. Now, Nick was doing much better, but he'd be taking his World History and Physical Science tests orally. Tam Turner. He'd taught Tam's older brother and sister, Jack and Liz. Good family. Nice kids.

"Excuse me. Could you please tell me how to get to Room 232?" The girl, looking lost, carried a huge book bag. Every year, the students looked younger and younger. Maybe it was just that he was getting older.

"This is Room 232," he answered, pointing to the numbers above his classroom door. "Come in and have a seat." He pointed to a chair. "What's your name?"

"Molly Manchester. I think my friend, Tam Turner, is in this homeroom too." Two boxes of pencils spilled from her book bag, splattering all over the floor. "Sorry!" she cried. "I'm just nervous."

Mr. Fell helped her retrieve the pencils, asking, "Do I know your family, Molly? Do you have any older brothers or sisters?" He didn't recognize any familial features in her face.

"Oh, no, sir. We just moved here a couple of years ago. My dad's in the army. He's stationed at the old post." Molly was beginning to feel a little more comfortable.

"Mr. Fell! My main man!" Mat Miller and Mr. Fell had been friends for a long time. Mat worked at his father's market, Chick's Fish Shack, after school and on weekends. Mr. Fell stopped at Chick's every Friday to buy fish. Always catfish. It was his favorite. And every time he bought it, he said the same thing: "Mat, when you get married, marry a girl who can cook. I married a cook and she makes the best catfish in the world!"

"So how's your employer, Mat?" That's what Mr. Fell always said when he asked Mat about his dad. Mr. Fell said corny things, but the kids all loved him. He tried to recognize each of his students as an individual.

The classroom was filling up. They had forms to fill out. There would be questions. Mr. Fell began with roll call so there would be time for the group to fill out all of these information forms for the office. The first year he'd taught, there had been just the list. Years later, information forms had become tougher than tests.

At some point, the school had begun using these complicated scanable sheets for information. This was supposed to expedite everything because the computer could handle voluminous information faster. "Strange," he mumbled to himself, "how something that's supposed to speed up a task makes it take so much longer."

Mr. Fell had never mastered the computer. All of his own children had learned, but the idea of having a machine in charge of his work made him uneasy. His wife always told him he was behind the times.

"I'll pass out these forms. You need a pencil, just come up here and get one. Or just ask Molly here.

She has enough to keep your whole class in pencils all the way through high school." He passed out the forms, saying, "Last name first, then first name, then middle name last. Press hard on the pencil. Don't use a pen. Fill in each one of these little bubbles in the right place, or we might not be able to figure out who you are. Might lose you."

While they began filling out their forms, he stared out the windows again. Football practice had already begun, but he would not be coaching this year. This would be the first time in more than 30 years that he hadn't had the responsibility of head football coach.

His old assistant coach was taking over. Mr. Fell would serve in an advisory capacity during his last year at JHS. They hadn't actually asked him to leave. But he'd understood. And letting go had been hard.

It had been the grayest day he'd ever known, the day he cleaned his personal belongings from the JHS locker room in July. But he knew that he had to let Bill Stromeyer take over. Bill had to feel free to make his own decisions. Football was like that. Two people couldn't be in charge.

Students were handing him their forms, but he was in a sort of daze. He hadn't heard the bell that sounded, signaling them to go to their 1st period classes.

"We're going to miss having you for our coach," young Sam Webster was saying to him. "My dad says you're the finest coach this school ever had, and he's sorry I won't be lucky enough to work with you."

"Well, thanks, Sam. It's nice of your dad to say that. Tell him I said hello." Mr. Fell was overcome by the full realization of how much his life would change this year. He had always spent every autumn afternoon and evening with his football players. Even when it stormed, they would work indoors, 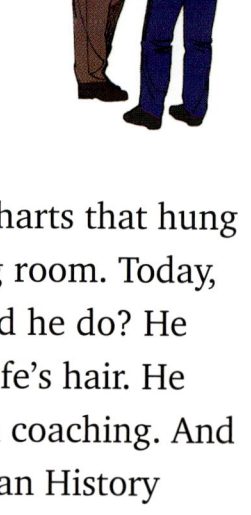 plotting Xs and Os on the big play charts that hung in the athletic department's meeting room. Today, he'd be finished at 3:15. What would he do? He couldn't go home. He'd get in his wife's hair. He didn't feel old enough to retire from coaching. And as for his World History and American History classes, he could teach them with his hands tied behind his back. History, after all, never changed. Only people changed. They got old.

"Mr. Fell, I don't get this." Tam Turner looked confused. "It says on my computer printout:

homeroom, Room 232. Then it says, 1st period, Room 232. Do you think it's a mistake?"

"It's not a mistake, Tam. It means you stay here for first period. You're in my World History class. There are probably a bunch of others from homeroom who were supposed to stay here, since this class is required. They'll be back, once they figure out they're lost. You've got a few minutes, if you need to get to your locker."

Tam really liked Mr. Fell. He made her feel comfortable. She remembered being riddled with worry just this morning, nervous about her first day of high school. "Mr. Fell, I wondered if I should ask you. Do you think . . . I mean, I know you're probably too busy, but I was wondering. . . ."

"Busy? No. Do I have time? Yes. All the time in the world. What can I do you for?" Tam recalled her older sister Liz and Liz's friends, laughing about how Mr. Fell was always saying, "what can I do you for." They could even imitate the way he said it.

"A couple of us are running for office. We worked all summer on our posters and raps. I have to give a speech next week in front of the whole school. Do you think you'd be able to listen to it? Like, maybe give me some advice about how I could spruce it up?"

Tam knew that Mr. Fell helped students with things like this; both Liz and her older brother, Jack, had been student council reps when they had been JHS students. Much to her surprise, he remembered.

"Would you believe I listened to your brother Jack and sister Liz both practice their first student council speeches? You Turners are some orators. As I told Jack, it is probably because there are six kids in your family, each kid has to be an orator to be heard!" Mr. Fell chuckled at his own joke.

At 7:30 the next morning, Mr. Fell was in the huge, silent auditorium with Tam and Sid North. Sid, it turned out, was running for class president.

Mr. Fell took Tam and Sid into the sound booth to show them how to control the audio system and how to use their lavaliere mikes. "The idea is," he said, "to look confident and show leadership. When you have a sound problem, you can't do that." He had seen good presentations ruined. He had seen student candidates lose because of things they hadn't been prepared for.

Sid went first. His speech was magnificent. Sid's huge baritone voice filled the auditorium. "I knew it," Mr. Fell thought to himself. "This boy has what it takes. We've got a leader here."

"OK, Tam. Your turn. Sid, you come sit down here and take notes. You can give her some advice, too. Let's go. Homeroom starts in twenty minutes." While Tam delivered her speech, Mr. Fell began taking notes. He would spend two or three more mornings with her. She'd be fine. Probably not a political leader, but fine.

Earlier, Sid had asked Mr. Fell about helping another student, a candidate for something. Treasurer? He'd said yes, he'd help that one too. He didn't mind. He always got up at 5:00 every morning anyway.

"All right, you two. I'm going into the teachers' lounge and grab a quick cuppa java before homeroom. See you in a few minutes!" Mr. Fell was off. You'd never know his age by the way he moved.

Sid looked at Tam. "What in the world is a cuppa java?"

Tam shrugged her shoulders. "You got me. He's a funny guy. He's not the hippest teacher in this school, but there's something about him I just like."

"You know my cousin Douglas? The runner? Placed second in the state in cross country? He said Mr. Fell wasn't even his coach, but he helped him out every Saturday before the state meet. Mr. Fell could hardly stand it when Douglas won. He was as excited as Doug's own mother!" Sid told Tam how Mr. Fell had singled him out last spring after the Martin Luther King speech contest. Mr. Fell had encouraged him to run for office.

"Shoot," Sid said to himself. "He probably doesn't even remember that." But Sid remembered. He'd never forget it. The older man had spoken so sincerely that Sid knew he wasn't jiving. He was serious about Sid having what he'd called "leadership potential."

Tam Turner stepped up to the podium. This was it. The day. Molly had offered her new dress, but Tam had decided to wear her own instead. They weren't the richest people in town, but her clothes were decent. She wore the bluish gray jean dress her mom had made her last summer.

September was one of the hottest months, and the school didn't have air conditioning. Tam felt a drop of perspiration trickling down her back. There was Mr. Fell, sitting in the front row, giving her a big smile. If she got nervous, she was supposed to look at him.

Waiting for her signal to begin, Tam thought of what her dad had said last night, as she practiced her speech one last time. "Don't worry about Liz and Jack both being in student council. You're not them. You're you. We know you'll do just fine. As long as you try, that's all we care about."

"Stand up straight," her mother had said. "People who slouch look like they don't care. Just remember to stand up straight, and you'll do fine."

Tam stood up as straight as she could. She remembered a little trick Liz had taught her. "Make the biggest space you can between your rib cage and your pelvis. It will straighten out your whole body."

A voice spoke through the auditorium speakers. "Our first candidate this morning, Tam Turner, is running for student council representative." That was Tam's signal to begin.

When it was over, Tam could barely remember. It didn't seem like ten minutes. She had never realized before what a lot of preparation went into a ten-minute speech. Yet, when she had actually delivered the speech, it felt as though only a few seconds had gone by.

Just once, she'd gotten stuck. But she'd looked down in the front row. With an encouraging smile, Mr. Fell gave her some soundless applause. She'd started right in again; her friends said they hadn't even noticed.

Mr. Fell was standing at the door of his classroom, clad in his red striped tie, waiting to greet the students as they arrived. Some of the younger teachers wore jeans, but Mr. Fell always wore a tie and a jacket. He knew some of his colleagues thought he was old-fashioned. Maybe he was. But he still believed that gentlemen dressed properly for work. Besides, he had to provide a role model for his students.

Everybody was chatting about the speeches they'd heard in assembly. This was election day, so it would be a half-day. There would just be the assembly, which took up most of the morning, and then homeroom. During homeroom, they were to fill out their ballots. Then lunch. After lunch, everybody would go home.

Both Tam and Sid felt apprehensive. Their friends all said encouraging things, but they both knew that their opponents' speeches had been good. They had spent the first two weeks of school campaigning. Today, after the others left, the candidates were responsible for staying until they had removed all their campaign signs from the hallways and classrooms.

"I can't believe it's over," Tam confided to Kim Chung. "Thanks for helping with my campaign song, Kim. I really appreciate all your help. You know that whenever you need something, all you have to do is ask me. You and Molly were champs! Without her posters and your song, I wouldn't have had a campaign."

Time flew. Before she realized it, Tam's friends were gone and the halls were nearly silent. Sam Webster, who had managed her campaign and Sid's, along with two other students', stayed to help remove signs, but he couldn't stay long. "Sorry,

Tam. I gotta go. Coach says if we're late, we're benched for the next game. You were great."

"Thanks, Sam," Tam replied, a little teary. "You've done enough. Really. I guess I'll see you later this afternoon. We have cheerleading practice."

Since they had been children, there had been a thing about Sam and Tam. They had played on the same T-ball team. They had been in the same class every year since first grade. Their parents knew each other. But now, Tam's feelings about Sam were changing a little. She thought his might be, too. It was the way he touched her arm when he left for football practice. Something about the way he looked at her. Her spine felt tingly.

She was exhausted. Wearily, she carted the last of her piles of posterboard and masking tape off toward the recycling center at the end of the first floor's west wing. Smiling, Tam remembered her first few days at JHS, when she'd thought she'd never learn her way around this huge building.

On her way to her locker on the second floor, Tam heard someone calling to her. "Miss Turner!" She looked around and saw Mr. Fell waving at her from the door of the teachers' lounge. Mrs. Chung stood there next to him. Tam knew that since they were both class sponsors, they'd be counting the votes for her class. But she knew better than to say anything about it. She'd have to wait until tomorrow, like everybody else.

"Hi, Mr. Fell! Hi, Mrs. Chung!" Scurrying toward her locker, Tam Turner realized that there was something about this place that she liked very much, very much indeed. And she realized that it didn't really matter who won the student council election.

Later, as she walked across the street toward the football field, clad in her sweats for cheerleading practice, Tam noticed Mr. Fell sitting idly in his car, watching the players on the varsity football field. "That's strange," she thought to herself. I wonder what he's doing there?" She waved at him, dashing to catch up with her friends.

Sitting there in his dilapidated car, the old historian's thoughts turned to his new students. What would become of them? In the blink of an eye, they would graduate. Work. Have families. Have joys and sorrows. Retire. He felt time

marching. At once, he had a clear vision of truth: nothing ever changed. He returned once more to other students from the past, some parents of the ones he'd met today. He would never forget any of them. And they would never forget him.

Vocabulary Expansion

Describe and define these words and phrases:

a winner never quits and a quitter never wins

running for	scanable sheets	look confident
head coach	swarm of students	baritone voice
a rewarding career	the grayest day	political leader
familial features	in a daze	cuppa java
my main man	plotting Xs and Os	hippest
employer	get in his wife's hair	you got me
corny jokes	hands tied behind his back	jiving
roll call	what can I do you for	podium
letting go	spruce it up	singled him out
take over	audio system	teachers' lounge

Language Expansion Activities

1. (a) Write an essay about a teacher or another person who has affected your life in some positive way; or (b) Write an essay about a teacher or another person who has affected your life in some negative way.

2. Organize a debate. Split into two groups, Affirmative and Negative. Use the following proposition: *Teachers should assist their students in extracurricular activities as well as class activities.*

Language Expansion Questions

1. Why was this a special year for Mr. Fell? What was the one regret he had about his new group of homeroom students?

2. Molly told Mr. Fell that she was "a little nervous." Explain why.

3. What prompted Sid North to run for class president? Do you think he would win? What does Mr. Fell think about Sid? How has Mr. Fell affected Sid's life? Has anyone ever affected you that way?

4. Explain the pressure Tam's family had unwittingly placed on her. How do you think she felt when her father told her it didn't matter whether she won? Do you think it relieved the stress she felt?

5. Sam's father made a comment about Mr. Fell. Sam told Mr. Fell what his dad had said. How did this affect Mr. Fell? Think of something someone told you that had a profound effect on you.

6. People within a community can have a profound effect upon each other and upon their community. For some, like Mr. Fell, it's not a single incident, but the way they live their daily lives that makes a difference to others. Discuss things you might do that could have a profound effect upon your community.

7. Sid North said that Mr. Fell probably didn't remember that he had encouraged Sid to run for office last spring. Did Mr. Fell remember? How do you know?

8. Make predictions about what will happen to the students in Mr. Fell's homeroom. Explain your predictions.

9. What one thing is the biggest worry to each of the students in the story? How do you know? Is it possible for someone who appears confident to be riddled with worry? Do you believe that all people harbor secret fears? Defend your position.

10. What is the theme of this story? Put it into sentence form. Is it universal? Explain.